Your Living Family Tree

Keeping your family together forever through print, photos, sound, and video

Gordon Burgett

ISBN 978-0-9796295-4-9 (Print version)
ISBN 978-0-9796295-5-6 (Adobe version)

Published by Communication Unlimited, P.O. Box 845, Novato, CA 94948 / (800) 563-1454. For details, see www.yourlivingfamilytree.com.

Other books by Gordon Burgett

Niche Publishing: Publish Profitably Every Time!
Travel Writer's Guide (3rd ed.)
How to Plan a Great Second Life! (2nd ed.)
Treasure and Scavenger Hunts (3rd ed.)
Empire Building by Writing and Speaking
Niche Marketing for Writers and Speakers
How to Set Up/ Market Your Own Seminar (audio CD)
Creating Your Own Audio CDs (audio CD)

Ordering information and full details available at
www.gordonburgett.com

Table of Contents

Table of Contents (2)

Section 5   # The Future

Appendix

Table of Contents (3)

Dedication,
Acknowledgements,
and
Gratitude

This book is dedicated to Barbara Ivy,
who has filled my life with a special joy and new meaning.

Barbara and many others have made this book fun to write.

Tamara Lipori chipped a dormant and unrooted idea loose in my mind in a follow-up conversation to a program I had just offered a couple of years ago in Santa Rosa, California, and we followed that up with a brainstorming afternoon at a local pizzeria. She's an expert on scrapbooking, and her helping me understand that medium better let me see the core concept that this book suggests in a different and more applicable light.

My special gratitude also goes to brother Jim Burgett, sister Nikki Burgett, daughter Shannon Graydon, and close friends Lu Hintz, Fred and Carol Adams, Angela M. Orlando, and Linda Lange, all of whom offered valuable suggestions as this book was being written. The inevitable errors, alas, are mine.

Introduction

We only get so many years of happiness, giving, and love on this earth, then we're gone. Sorry. A hundred years from now all that most of us will be is a name and a few myths...

We'll be like Great Aunt Maude who might have been a spinster or maybe Uncle Albert's mother, and is she buried in Grand Rapids or Chicago?

We may as well write our lives in invisible ink!

Forget all the fun and the good deeds and sacrifices. Forget that every one of our lives is unique and singular. That we work hard and are kind to dogs and widows and that we deserve to be remembered. Poof and we're hundred-year dust!

Wouldn't it be great if we could reverse that?

What if we could select what our great-great-great-grandchildren know about us? What if we could share forever our awe at seeing our children born, the horror of experiencing 9/11, what it was like to win the spelling bee—or anything heartfelt at the moment it took place?

Then let's do it!

It's the 21st century, the miracle era of easy and inexpensive digital preservation. There's no reason that we and every living member of our family can't leave a written, visual, oral, and active presence of our own choosing to be enjoyed, appreciated, and learned from by both present family members and offspring far into the future!

There's no reason we can't create our own Living Family Tree, planted this week and fed and trimmed for the next 100, 200, 500, or 1,000 years by our kids, their kids, and so on…

To do that we need a structure around which we can build the family exchange, we must give it continuity, and we need a process by which all family members (who wish to) can participate in and preserve the new project almost forever.

Bingo. That's what this book describes!

Let's create and plant a family tree that will unite all of the members from this day forward.

But not an old-fashioned, one-dimensional family tree limited to lists of dead kin. That tree points backward and downward, until the roots disappear. We need a "living family tree" that starts today, points upward and forward, is open-ended, and invites participation by every family member and generation yet to come.

Then the old-fashioned family tree can be included, a much researched root revered by the family living now and yet to come. The future research will be a lot easier: we, while we are alive, will provide it.

But let's also fill our new living family tree with sound, written memories, digital photos, videos, and things made or worn by our family. Let's inject all of the living senses we can capture and keep them alive, at least digitally, forever!

Let's hear your thoughts at five, see you and your sisters joking around the Christmas tree, watch you play basketball on the school team, later read your dissertation, then your book, see your family grow, watch the entirety of your life unfold—now or 250 years from now.

Best yet, that new-millennial tree with 100 more lives like yours would be instantly and forever accessible at any hour to any family member because it's planted as close as the nearest computer.

Are there other benefits beyond immortality?

At least a baker's dozen plus six, as you'll see later. Let me talk about one benefit particularly worth sharing at the outset.

If you could help a cousin still to be born 100 years in the future live a much better life, or stay out of trouble, or do something extraordinary just because of an example you left in print (or by audio or video), would that get your attention?

And if the situation were reversed and you were desperately seeking some guidance or an up-from-the-bootstraps example, you were looking at the "living family tree," and there was something inspirational from some cousin who lived 130 years earlier... You get the idea.

A "living family tree" with everybody contributing during their life has so much more potential than just keeping us eternally waving at relatives. It lets each member of the extended family share their life, heart, and experiences with every other member somewhere in time.

How does all of this happen?
Who sets it up?
Who keeps the website family tree fertilized and growing?
How can we join in?
Is changing the direction of family history really this easy?

Read on...

A family tree can wither if nobody tends to its roots.

A Great New Idea, a Vision, and the Benefits

Let me share a great new idea just popping out of the 21st century. *You* can easily and quickly create *your own* "living family tree"!

You know what a regular family tree is. It tells about your folks' families, and their families: when and where they were born, who they married, information about their kids, and when and where they died.

Family trees usually go back until the roots disappear or get murky. They're fun to read to see if there were knights or dukes among your kin—or if a horse thief was hanging from a stout branch!

But what if you could create a tree that started right now, grew forward for 100 or 1000 years, and drew every one of your living relatives—or yet to live—into a warm, tightly-bound clan?

You can. And you have almost every tool at hand because of the extraordinary electronic revolution we are experiencing.

The old-fashioned family tree is a real treasure but it has been limited to recording past dates and places, with a few tattered tintypes pasted in. Today, we can collect the actual words and actions (almost the souls) of every member of your family through sound, video, podcasts, .jpgs, and digital writing. Most important, everything collected can be easily organized and preserved, exactly as it is, to be instantly enjoyed by your cousin across the world or by your great-grandson's cousin 60 or 100 years from now, after he is born and looking back to see what his ancestors (that's you!) thought and did.

That's about as close to magic as we can get. This book will give you the how-to details.

A Vision and Some Benefits

We need a plan, a vision, around which to create a living family tree. It's your tree and you can design it any way you wish. But for starters, let's imagine that your tree includes

* a core couple
* a director
* a nuclear website
* many information-sharing locations on the website
* a related email link for family members to submit information
* a submission guideline to provide some structural protocol for those submissions
* a family-shared plan for development and continual use of your living family tree
* perhaps a Family Board to help design and maintain the project
* possible family reunions to physically bring the living members together and expand the reach and sense of the living family tree

But first, why would you and your family even want a living family tree? Because it

* acknowledges the existence and importance of each member of each branch of your direct family and it directly links you to each of them
* lets each member share their personal thoughts, contributions, and achievements with other members of the living family
* conveys the sense of accomplishment and worth shared by each member
* provides to each relative while they are living or after they have passed a kind of historical intimacy (through voice, video, picture, and word)
* calls attention to the core family values that span the generations
* extends a sense of worth to every family member by having actively contributed to a family team project
* provides current, quickly updated family contact information
* accessibly preserves your family history in one place
* widely shares family-based wisdom and humor
* instils both family and personal pride and unity

There's more too. A living family tree will provide a form of interwoven, intergenerational immortality. As long as the tree blooms, or exists, every family member can continue to live in the minds of those they love, through their achievements, pictures, writings, voice, and words. The tree can provide solace for the lonely, a buttress in grief, and an inspiration from others who succeeded to those needing succour, support, or encouragement. It could provide laughter, memories, and awe in children seeing themselves celebrated to their clan. And nobody in the family will be truly lost, forgotten, or unembraced.

Why hasn't anybody thought of this before? For the same reason that nobody thought of retooling genes before we

knew about DNA or nobody broadcast the Olympics before we
had radio or TV!

Of course, somebody has to get the living family tree going. They must sow the first seed. Trees, however extraordinary, can't plant themselves!

Do you want to be a legitimate family hero, revered for
the next 100 or 500 years by your own flesh and blood? Plant
the seed.

The idea is so new and makes so much sense somebody in
your line is going to be the pioneer. We know that you already
have more than enough wit and intelligence. All that's missing
is the know-how, and we'll help there.

You'll be the hero because you grasped the magic and had
the gumption and tenacity to make it work for those you love
most! Keep reading.

If you're not the heroic type? Just send it to the smartest,
bravest person in your family. Let them pick up the accolades,
with of course a sage nod your direction for having made the
first suggestion! One thing's certain: your family will love having their own living family tree.

Think forward to see why that seed should be planted
now. Not only will it start with a living couple (you or your
parents?), it will multiply every time someone in your family
has a child. Who knows how many branches it will have in
200, 500, or 1000 years. Best yet, if started now, you will be
included, and gratefully thanked, by every one of those new
family members. And what will they know about you? Everything you wish to share in words, photo, song, video, or artefacts.

But I'm getting ahead of myself.

The Parts

It couldn't be simpler. We are standing on *terra incognita*. Nobody knows what a perfect living family tree is yet. None exists as I write these words.

That's because this tree grows from mental seeds that are free of genetic restraints, so new genes (or mutations) are as easy to create as changing a word or stretching a vision.

You create your own living family tree. You are encouraged to graft new branches or change those configurations at will

If that's scary—you didn't expect to have to invent!—then let me suggest some parts of a living family tree that might serve as starting models or a framework that you can use, shrink, expand, combine, brighten, or even ignore.

What comprises a viable, long-lasting living family tree?

My concept has a **Family Tree Website**, a sort of digital trunk with branches, at its core and the most important long-term foundational information (think of leaves) in its **Personal Information Repository**.

Keeping track of your tree family (those included from the core couple forward) is probably best done with a **Family Di-**

rectory, with at least their vital contact information while they live, and the site of their grave (or remains) once they pass.

Another segment might be a **Key Date List**, which tells for the current year (or 12 months out) the birthdates, baptism dates, anniversaries, family reunion details, coming graduations and marriages, and anything else of a date nature pertaining to the living members.

A longer-term unit (from the start of the tree into the far future) might be a **Family Registry**, where each birth, baptism, marriage, and death will be registered. That might also be extended backward to include provable keystone events for those in the Ancestral Family Tree.

"Tip of the Hat" Acclamations are family hurrahs in webtalk that herald significant achievements that all of the kin should know about. What's significant? That's the core question that the Director or Family Board must decide, but key promotions, degrees or certificates received, offices held, publications, and inventions produced are the kinds of unique and laudatory accomplishments that are surely worthy of familial ovation.

Alas, one also takes off their hat for the **"In Memoriam" Announcement**, which honors the passing of a family member, which might include a short biography, photo, key details, and commentary about the person from family and friends.

An **Annual Family Summary** might do just as it states, summarize for that year the happy and sad news shared by those in the tree family.

The **Family Treasures in Print** and **Family Treasure Box** are locations where important relics are stored, to be seen and appreciated or even taken out, handled, admired—and returned! The first will hide at the website, where copies of items like articles, books, scores, and patents can be viewed in original or scanned form. The second will hide in a family member's dry storeroom, to be taken to reunions and gatherings, the core of later family museum holdings.

Family Flashes are really email announcements sent to those eager to be on the instant recipient list of news of great family importance, like a birth, death, or other momentous happenings that should be conveyed quickly.

The **Ancestral Family Tree** is really the old-fashioned family tree limited to the core couple's direct descendants. It will move backward chronologically while the living family tree moves forward, and it may employ much of the same structure and formats (with words, photos, sounds, and even videos) while it provides links with the past.

A journey of far greater distance and breadth can be shared by individual family tree members through their written (or spoken) **Journals**, **Diaries**, or **Memoirs**, which can be forever accessible through the Family Website.

Scrapbooks can provide a fun, artistic slice-of-life look at any of the family tree members, particularly at occasions like notable birthdays or weddings. They could be preserved digitally or kept in the Family Treasure Box.

Unforgettable Recollections help all share what they were doing and thinking at key historical times.

Even, as they become affordable (and perhaps more understandable), copies of the DNA of family members might be kept on file.

What's missing is a how-to manual that tells the scattered family how they can share their facts, dreams, achievements, and treasures with the LFT (Living Family Tree) Director, and thus with the family. So a **Family Submission Guide** might be a valuable helper to demystify the contribution process.

Those are some obvious ways that today's family facts can be sorted into usable components that could link us to any of our family members at any time now or in the future.

Don't pass out or flee! You can have a great living family tree with just one or two components. Or you can introduce three at the outset, and add a new part annually. The most important thing is to get something started now, then build from that base.

Later we will see why *right now* is the best time ever to compile a living family tree, since we can easily expand it beyond words to include photos, sound, and video. Better yet, we can freeze anything we gather, store it, and make it instantly accessible to any other relative eager to share it anywhere else in the world. Wow!

The Nuclear Website

To most people, the prospect of creating one's own website is scary enough to sink the whole project before it even gets afloat. In truth, it's not that big a deal or everyday people and tiny companies wouldn't have one.

A website is after all just one big file that sits in some company's back room hundreds or thousands of miles (but digital microseconds) away that can be read by as many people as you want from the comfort (one hopes) of their own home or office. It only shows what you put in that file. You are the gateway to what the others can see.

Let's break that down into digestible bytes, and assure you that there are lots of people along the way eager to help you succeed in creating a super site that will be the pivotal medium for your family's living history.

Here are a few starter website truths:

* Websites that the public uses are almost always identified by a name followed by .com, .net, .org, or other dot-something (sometimes even followed by another dot-something, usually indicating a country).
* Each website "rents" its name.

* You pay a fee to a company that guarantees that name for the time chosen.

* The group from whom you rent the site should inform you well in advance of the loss date, though to be safe you should keep track of that date as well, contacting the company a month or so before the expiration occurs.

* You can continue to use that name indefinitely as long as you pay the fee before a certain surrender date.

* You can determine the length of rental time (minimally a year, often two or three) and the amount of space its contents use.

The space for www.yourlivingfamilytree.com, for example, was rented from a server that I've never met but with whom I have regular protocol contact. When they tell me that the name rental is due to expire in a couple of months (as they have faithfully done with the many websites we have with them), I renew it for two more years. The actual server space is ours until we decide to move the contents elsewhere or the server throws us out. Nobody else can use that name and every time I check my website on my computer it is just where I left it and it looks just the same!

Let's say that your family name is Smiles and the Smiles Living Family Tree Board decides to call your website www.smilesfamilytree.com because it's easy to remember and is a clear description of why the site exists. But before you start using that name, you must first check to see if somebody else is already using it or if some firm has reserved it. To do that, you simply type the name, http://www.smilesfamilytree.com into your Internet entry and see what appears. If somebody else's website pops up, it's in use.

If www.smileslivingfamilytree.com is another choice, try that.

If this message appears, "We are unable to locate the server www.smileslivingfamilytree.com. The server does not have a DNS entry," that probably means that nobody has registered that particular website.

Visit http://www.internic.net/whois.html to be doubly sure. That is where all registered sites are said to be found. If it still doesn't show an owner, register it immediately! That gives you a place for your living family tree to grow roots! All that remains is to pay the fee so the site is yours forever. You can easily change your server (or even the website name) later on.

Some naming suggestions: (1) Give your website a name that your family can easily find and remember; it's best to put the shared surname somewhere in it; (2) Avoid putting hyphens in your website name (like www.smiles-family-tree.com) because it is so easy for the family members (now and later) to forget to insert the hyphens, (3) Avoid using the number "1" and the letter "l" in the title since they look almost identical, and (4) Most people automatically type in .com as the ending. If you had selected .org or .net, though, typing in .com won't connect to your website. So, if the site is available, use .com.

Then you start with some friendly software...

Now that you have a website name, you need something to put on it and a way to get it there!

That's where it gets tougher, unless you are already comfortable creating websites, thinking in .html, and transporting text, photos, and audio content from your computer to the server's through a protocol system.

That's all learnable and doable, of course, and it can be no less definitive and accessible whether you do it, a Director acts as the conduit for the family and creates the basic transferable information with a server, or you or a Director use specialized software to expedite the whole process.

Check our website for information about website software programs created for living family trees.

How might your initial website appear?

Let's dismiss whirling circles, 127 colors, blinking boxes, and a full photo of every living family member on the face page right now and think of the simplest, most functional opening page. All the rest, heavens forefend, can come later!

Most opening pages (called the index) tell who you are, why you are there, and how the viewer can contact you. Yours might say:

> ### SMILES LIVING FAMILY TREE

Let's say that the Director wants to begin with four sections in the Smiles living family tree. So below the title might appear a simple two-column box like this, under the word

DIRECTORY

The Smiles family	The personal page of every family member born since 1950
Family Directory	How to contact the listed Smiles family members
Key date list	Birthdays, anniversaries, and other important Smiles dates
"In Memoriam"	An honor page of Smiles family members who have passed on

The titles in the first column might also be highlighted, which will tell the viewer that each column is linked to a more complete explanation, if activated.

Since you may not want all information accessible to the public (for example, members' addresses and phone/fax/email numbers), when the person links to the second-level page (like the "Family Directory") it might explain the section in detail but then add "Viewing this page requires the use of a password."

Family members will all have the password, and will simply type it into a box to see the "Family Directory." Others won't know the password so the actual Directory will be hidden. You might also have a link on that page that asks "Did you forget your password?" The link will be an email form addressed to the Director. So if the email comes from forgetful old Aunt Lilly, she gets her password again (for the fifth time!) If it's a junk mailer, tough luck.

At the bottom of the index page you will surely want to type in at least the Director's name and contact link. So under the Directory might appear:

> **Smiles Living Family Tree Director**
> Lora Smiles
> (Lora@smilesLFT.com)

Go to www.yourlivingfamilytree.com/Smilesindex.htm if you want to see how this opening, or index, page might actually look on your computer,

Though this first page is as dull as sandpaper graphically, there's some wisdom in building a website like a medieval castle, with all the beauty and hidden treasure inside!

The directory will be much longer over time, but the glue that makes the project worthwhile and fun is on the many hidden pages yet to be read. Can it at least be prettier? You bet. The background could be in different colors and shades and the type, different fonts. You can hang the family shield or the coat of arms somewhere on the page, with flowers or smiling do-dads in the corners.

But don't add much artwork, like the core couples' picture or a string of snapshots of the ancestral plantation, on the open-ing page. Every decoration takes space and time to download, and that means it takes the user more time for the website to appear on their screen. Too much time and nobody will use it at all. Put the big, slow-to-download files (like photos, audio, video, and scanned objects) on the inside pages. The index should open almost instantly. Five seconds will seem like five minutes.

How do you add more information inside?

In the shortest of explanations, the website is the one file I am describing now. Everything else is a link from the index to another page, and on that second page you might also have one or many links to other pages or photos, and, yes, some of those will also continue linking. Sounds overwhelming but it really isn't.

For example, the first item in the directory above, The Smiles family, would be highlighted (usually underlined and in a different color). That is a link to a different page. If you click on that link with your mouse, it will take you to the actual al-phabetized members of the Smiles family. If Lora Smiles is listed, her name too will be highlighted (another link), and you could continue probing to greater depth about Lora. Some pages continue to link 5-50 times!

This is the point where the Director lifts the programming burden from your shoulders. The Director will tell you, for ex-ample, which facts should be listed in the "Family Directory" for each branch (and member) of the grander Smiles family.

How you will list those facts will be explained in that submission guideline. That would likely consist of a list of items needed after which you type in the data. Then you email that to the Director as an email text or an attachment, and that's it! (See the "Family Directory" example in the Appendix.)

The Director will convert the information you send to a software format, save it on his/her hard drive, and send it to the website server. In a few seconds it will be visible in Virginia and Vietnam!

Do you have a say in how the website looks?

Almost as much as you want if you are that saint known as the Director!

But plenty too as just a family member and contributor. Get on the Family Board and most of the design and structure will pass that way. Or take advantage of the requests that the Director will make on the submission guidelines and in most communications for comments and suggestions.

The success of your living family tree is directly related to the level and amount of buy-in from the family, and every idea, comment, or suggestion is one more element of that buy-in.

The Director's goal is to get the website up and running quickly and smoothly, then let it shift into a more predictable long-range flow, with the occasional reminder of its existence enough to keep it sustained and supported for decades, then centuries. Once it is up, the key dream is that through regular participation and support by all it will become part (maybe even the spine and banner) of that family's tradition.

Your living family tree is a website that brings alive and maintains vibrant every member from today forward. Comments and suggestions are a key part of that, almost as important as regularly providing the core data and up-dated life observations, photos, and spoken thoughts.

See the examples in the Appendix

It's easier to envision examples when there are models to view, so in the Appendix there are 17 models of how a starter living family tree might actually look. The examples are very plain and straightforward. The contents are the key element of each. How those contents are packaged offers 100 paths to fun. Have fun!

As my family planted for me, so do I plant for my children.

Talmud

The Ways

What's unique today is not only can we share and indefinitely retain a ton of instantly accessible information about our family, we can do it so many different ways!

In the old days, like in the 1990s, it was assumed that anything "family tree"-like would be a list of words in print, plus a few scattered photos and maybe a rare reel-to-reel tape recording.

What a change! Not only are we reversing the direction, by planning forward, there is so much diversity that half of our task is just staying ahead of the emerging technology.

Of course that still means our old friends written words, but words now instantly visible at any time and kept that way (relatively safe from prankish alteration) just about forever.

It also means photos, lots of them, visible without having to haul around film or an album; sounds at the tap of a finger, actual voices and music from a great-uncle's trumpet to your maiden aunts singing a duet, and videos. Relatives in the flesh, making noise, in motion!

So that's what section three is about. Capturing live people by many dimensions forever, as they live!

It really is a new world.

Words

Words are the bedrock of your living family tree. The data—birthdates, addresses, commentaries, kudos—are the bricks of this new building. So there's scarcely a reason for a separate chapter that tells you that the brick building you are standing in, looking at, or imagining is made of bricks.

But they have to be the right words—the right bricks. That is, they must be accurate. So the Director is on the prowl for birthdates in the right year (that year is so hard to remember as one ages!), the honor rolls achieved, and the correct degrees awarded.

And there must be enough of them. To get in the game and stay you have to ante up, so at key stages of your life, when you are dealt new hands, you have to share a bit of written prose to keep your Personnel Information Repository account current. The word bill occurs so seldom that the Director will likely send you a loving nudge. Please pay.

And they must be sent the right way. Or as close to the "right way" as you can. The medium is digital, so at some point the written words must, yes, be written, then transmitted electronically to the Director, who will convert them into usable software and send them to be stored almost forever, breaking them off into usable bits to share back with the family.

And they have to be in the right order. But here you have the greatest latitude because the Director can edit, patch, and trim. Just so they are understandable.

That's enough: the rest of the book tells what kinds of words are needed, why, and how to submit them. Yes, this is a tree made largely of bricks. Go figure.

Photos

If the saying is true about a photo being worth a thousand words, what would a sequence of nine photos of your contemporary family patriarch—or you—at the key stages of his life be worth to your great grandchildren, or their great-great grandchildren, or 600 years from now?

What if your Family Board requested that a digital photo of every family member be submitted at nine ages: birth, 5, 10, 15, 20, 35, 50, 65, and 80? And it promised, in exchange, to post those photos in your living family tree for all to enjoy?

Let's focus on that concept first, and some other photos too, before we talk about how they might be submitted.

Nine check-in times

Just a few years ago it was tedious and expensive to create photos. Cameras weren't cheap; you had to select the kind of photograph to send (black and white or color, print or slide, wallet-sized or 8x10); the only way to share it was on the wall, in a cut-and-paste scrapbook, or by mailing copies to kin; the negatives or slides scratched or deteriorated; photos faded, and so on.

What a change digital cameras and computers have made!

Acceptable cameras can be bought for less than $50. Some are even found in cell phones or on computer monitors! And the quality reproduction of a face they can create (even one as distinguished and of such stellar photographic eminence as your own) is better than adequate, and can even be touched up, brightened, shaded, or modified to be better yet.

What if the first photo misses your finest attributes, as hard as that is to imagine? Take another or a dozen until one is just right. Delete those of lesser superiority and the camera isn't offended, film isn't an issue, photo paper isn't wasted, and nary a dime is lost.

If that's not enough, that shot (or several) can be emailed to the Director or anybody else in a few seconds, and on the receiving end it (or they) can be opened up, viewed, expanded, resized, and/or touched up, then printed and/or saved. A thousand days (or 350 years) from now the same photo(s) can be opened and enjoyed again, all while copies of the digital original can be stored a hundred times on other, "safe" sites or backup CDs.

Most important, your best shot sits in the living family tree like a re-fleshed ornament, you eternally staring back at any person lucky enough to claim kinship—or at others less fortunate.

Why nine times? Because we all look remarkably different at key points during our lives and this is an opportunity to communally share a singular, never-to-be repeated manifestation of that growth.

Another blessing for those starting a living family tree now is that they can capture almost all of the family members at each of those age portals, and of all those yet born.

What about the others, like the core couple and the rest who have long pedalled their life cycles? They might be able to find earlier photos that match as closely as possible those age touch bases. (You can see how hard this would be if you were trying to do it in reverse with a traditional family tree. Tykes of five or ten were hardly worth photographing. In fact, most people before 1900 had one photo taken in their entire lives, at death! And much before Lincoln's time, none at all.)

Why not reduce that onerous request to four times? Or up it to 14? You and your family decide, but the nine times chosen are easy to remember, are well spaced to match major growth periods, and aren't so exact (within that year or thereabout) that a faulty memory or spate of procrastination will ruin the life display. The worst that will happen? There will be no photo at 10 or 40, which is precisely the same as if you never requested photos at set times at all. And the sun, we hope, will still keep shining.

What kind of photo? Head and shoulders only? Full body? Straight on or from a "best" side? Dressed in best duds or everyday digs? Wearing a hat or hatless? Just posing or doing something active? Vertical or square? Smiling or serious? If any of that is important, another family decision. One stipulation might apply, however: for the age shots, that it be of that person only. Not a group shot (unless, for those finding photos of earlier years, that's all that is available.)

Other photo opportunities

There are other times when individual photos would add considerably to the family photo font.

- Baptism, or a similar early religious activity or event
- Dramatic, musical, or community performances
- Key sports events: team photo(s), shooting the game-winning three pointer, skiing the Alps, catching for the Cubs, spiking a volleyball…
- Graduation
- Marriage (with the spouse)
- Receiving an award or recognition
- Other important opportunities

Many, as you can see, are "Tip of the Hat" occasions, where the photo might first appear.

Family photos are important too, with captions telling who the people are and their ages when photographed, as well as where the photo was taken and when.

Of particular importance would be multi-family group photos at events like large family gatherings, picnics, reunions, or other meetings. These might well merit a full-page spread in your living family tree with both the large group shot and an assortment of more informal, fun snapshots, with explanatory text.

How digital photos might be submitted

The Director will create a living family tree photo library, and from there will post the appropriate photos on the pages where they belong. (A few may rest on one page for a while, like a "Tip of the Hat" graduation photo, and will later be moved to another site, probably photo adjunct pages in your Personal Information Registry.)

Your job is to provide the photos in an easy-to-use format with the necessary factual captions and dates.

This process will change over time, but as this book is written it probably means that you (or somebody) will take the photos in question, then you will download your digital camera, most likely to your own computer, so you can review the photos and pick out the best to send to the Director. While .tif (or TIFF) photos are fuller and more comprehensive, they are also considerably bigger (which means they take up more space on a disc and take longer to download) than .jpg (or JPEG) photos, so it is in the latter format that the Director will ask that your photos be sent. (Most digital photos already emerge from the camera, in a manner of speaking, as .jpgs, ready to send.)

How will you send them to the Director? As an attachment to an email.

This is where the Family Submission Guide will provide the specifics—how you label each photos, how it is sent, captions needed, and the rest of the details.

Taking and sending photos has gotten so easy to do and so hard to goof up. And the photos will make a huge difference as time goes on. They will convert a text-heavy website into a fun venture of linking to full-form people. (Adding the person's spoken voice or seeing them in a video will add even more dimensions to this living digital scrapbook.)

The hardest part is simply remembering to take the photos at the appropriate times (the nine times and at the most important life moments), then sending them promptly to the Director so the good news and views can be shared simultaneously.

What if your photos are pre-digital?

If you are starting the living family tree now, in the age of digital photography, most of the pre-digital photos will be historical pictures of the past. And since in this book we have distinguished between the Ancestral Family Tree, which ends now but grows backward through the past, and the living family tree, which has its roots with a recent core couple (who are probably still living) and grows forward, again the pre-digital photos are much more likely to be needed for the historical family tree, and be only tangentially related to this book's main purpose.

Still, if you only have pre-digital photos, or if your living family tree also contains an Ancestral Family Tree, it is highly likely that the Director will either give you instructions about how to digitally submit your earlier photos or will simply have you carefully wrap them and physically send them so he/she can make the conversions in person.

Sounds

What did your great-grandmother sound like? Did she have a bellowing backwoods holler with a twang? Did she have the diction of a no-nonsense schoolmarm? Was she loquacious or scared to death that the recorder was capturing her soul?

And what did she have to say about life on the farm in 1906, or 1930? What were her earliest family recollections? About her grandfather talking about the Civil or Spanish-American War? How she met and captured your great-grandfather's heart? Her first flight in an airplane? Or how she got her first driver's license at 66?

And what about that brass band your father and his brothers had when they were rapscallions, did they ever record their playing? Want to share your daughter's flute rendition of the "Star Spangled Banner"? Or sing and preserve the song that your spouse wrote for a local musical?

The primary reason for creating an audio component as part of your living family tree is obvious: once digitally captured, it is available through the ages to be heard often and forever—or never. A voice or sound captured now simply affords a new way of relating to your kin later, and of repeatedly sharing their message and accomplishments.

A true vignette of lost opportunity makes the point more emphatically.

When Barbara Ivy, now from Marin County in California, was born in the late 1930s, her parents made their living by performing in a family "medicine show" in Missouri, complete with elixir (rumored to be prune juice and booze) for sale at the end of each performance! She was an Ussery then and even though her folks, with the children, moved to California soon after her birth, her father remembered, until his death in his 90s in 2005, every word of every routine he had performed. But it never occurred to anybody to have Harley record this valuable historical material, which he would have been pleased to do. So not only is her family deprived of sharing this intimate uniqueness, so is the greater tribe of social historians now and far into the future.

What sounds should be saved?

The roughest of guidelines might suggest at least one or two items from every living family member from now into the future, plus if an historical family tree is being preserved, anything oral from every directly-related relative that can be gathered from the past.

Add to that anything additional that has special worth, like the medicine show routines just mentioned or other utterances of value (such as valedictorian graduation speeches, appearances on radio or TV, talks to community groups or at conferences or conventions, and so on).

If every family member is to speak "on the record" at least twice, what are they expected to say?

Another Family Board decision, accepting as a sad fact there will probably be a maverick per decade or two who will flat-out refuse to follow any guideline at all. From them you may have to accept whatever they offer, as long as it's decent and not too embarrassing. Or you may have to play "Hidden Mic," then keep the results in the vault until they die from meanness or muleheadedness.

How can those sounds be saved?

Let's focus on a couple of oral contributions per family member, minimum, in their lifetime. (The mavericks must fend for themselves, until they see how much fun this can be.)

There are two formats that quickly suggest themselves—(A) an open-ended interview and (B) a question-driven interview—plus some mixture of the two (C).

And there are three obvious structures: (1) a one-voice presentation, (2) a two-voice program, and (3) a multi-voice recording.

Finally, you may want to ask the members to do the recordings at specific time periods in their life, to create some continuity (and tie-in with later kin at that same time period). That would also show change by that person over their years.

For example, the first recording might be done at about 15 years of age, with the second at 45. Subsequent, optional but valuable recordings might be made at 65 and 85 (or shortly before one's passing, as hard as that is to plan with precision).

Might there be times when family members should orally share additional, unique experiences and observations? You bet! Wouldn't it be extraordinary to hear what it was like to study and graduate from, say, West Point or Annapolis? Or wrestle or skate in the Olympics? Or to have fought in a particular battle or theater in a war, or to have just finished two years of Peace Corps or medical ministry in a critical place abroad? In fact, anything of exceptional import to any family member that they want to orally share should be openly embraced.

Perhaps some examples of (A)-(C) and (1)-(3) would make the above suggestions easier to comprehend. If the family wishes to strictly adhere to set formats and definite specific time periods, minimally, for recording, then the Family Board would have to make those decisions known.

Formats (A) to (C)

While (C), a mixture of the two, is self-explanatory, what is the difference between (A), an open-ended interview, and (B) a question-driven interview?

An open-ended interview begins with the simplest of guidelines, often one or several questions, and invites speakers to say whatever they wish in response, usually with the understanding that they are welcome to branch off at will whenever it enhances the worth of the communication.

Can the person just babble on forever? Unless the guidelines suggest an ideal length or put a time cap on the recording, I suppose so. Of course, others will stop listening if nothing of substance is being said or if the presentation isn't sufficiently entertaining.

What kind of questions might provoke an unencumbered free-flow response? Maybe these, or better ones that you or the Family Board might design:

- "What's life been like for you during your first 15 years, and how would you describe your life right now?"
- "At 15, what do you plan to do between now and, say, 45?"
- "At 45, what major life changes have occurred to you since you last recorded at 15? How would you describe your life right now?"
- "From a mid-life vantage point of 45, what have been the high and low points of your life so far, and what do you want to accomplish or do in your coming "second life"?
- Would you please share some advice for other family members, those joining the oral family tree at 15 or others at any age...

A question-driven interview is more tightly structured. It might contain 10-50 questions, each soliciting a rather specific answer of fairly short duration. Some of the questions seek purely factual responses ("At 45, what are the names of your children, their ages right now, and are they presently at home or living on their own?"). Others ask for opinion or observation ("Is your life less restrictive now, at 45, than it was when you were 15? If so, how? [Or if not, how?]").

(C) is some combination of opening or organizational questions, to gather specific factual or historically descriptive information, with some broad, open questions interspersed or at the end to stimulate the speaker to include his or her own thoughts, dreams, and admonitions.

Structures (1) to (3)

The three structures need little elaboration.

The one-voice presentation would find the person speaking alone into a microphone or recording device.

The two-voice program would most likely consist of one person, an interviewer, asking questions or guiding the discussion, with the other, the family member, responding. (How interesting this might be if a grandchild, say, interviewed a grandparent. Or the reverse.) Another two-person format might be of two family members both recording their voices and thoughts by talking to and with each other.

A multi-voice recording would be three or more voices on the same program. It might be an interviewer with, perhaps, a pair of grandparents recording together. Or it might be created at a table of family elders sharing memories or thoughts with each other (and an audience of live listeners) at the family reunion, with several microphones being used to capture all that is said. (A voice-over can later explain who each speaker is before or after the person talks.)

How do the members record their segments?

The recording tools would likely be a microphone connected to a computer, where the sound is stored; an internal digital storage component, battery-driven, into which a person (or people) can speak, or on an analog device, like a tape recorder that produces audio cassettes.

Let's discuss all three formats. Before using any of the three it is wise to at least have a rough idea of what you will talk about. In lieu of a word-for-word script, a list of topics or questions is more likely to give the result more order and a greater sense of purpose.

Recording by computer

To do this you need three things: a computer with a sound system that records, a speaker connected to the computer (usually one or two small white boxes, one with an on/off switch and volume control) so you can hear what you said, and a microphone that plugs into the back of the computer into which you speak (the plug-in hole is usually green and is near the plug that goes to the printer).

Assuming that you have recording software on your computer (almost all do) and a small microphone (it usually comes with the computer software), it's as simple as activating the sound recorder and then recording.

The Director will provide the actual step-by-step details in a Family Submission Guide.

Recording with a battery-driven hand device

As this book is being written these small, hand-held voice recorders are still new at an affordable price range. They provide the same kind of digital recording as a computer. The result can also be edited later or conveyed to the Director as is.

Using an Olympus WS-100 Digital Voice Recorder, for example, the person can either speak into the recorder itself or into an attached microphone. It is powered by a AAA alkaline 1.5 volt battery that lasts about 13 hours, and the device detaches from the battery to become a USB connection that will plug directly into the back of a computer, with the recording then downloadable into the hard drive. The sound volume can be controlled on the side of the recorder or at the microphone. It records 64 MB of sound in five folders that will contain up to 199 messages each.

To record, one slides the OFF/ON button to ON, then touches the RECORD button. It can be stopped at any time, and of course the sound can be heard back. (It also has a FAST FORWARD and REWIND button and a small action window that tells what the recorder is doing.)

The process is straightforward. You push the button, record what you wish, stop, plug it into your computer, download the recorded folder(s), and either edit the words (or music) or send them to the Director with only a format change.

What makes the small digital voice recorder a blessing to those creating a living family tree is that even the least technologically sophisticated in the family could be mailed the device, with a fresh battery, about four instructions, and three buttons to move or push. They record their offering and mail it back. It requires almost no mechanical or computer knowledge at all. In fact, every member of the family could record a segment and it could all be returned in the same 54-gram device!

Recording with a tape recorder that produces audio cassettes

This might be a more comfortable solution for many of the older readers of this book who are accustomed to using audio cassette recorders. But that has a built-in conflict for the LFT

Director: audio cassettes are recorded in analog and the other two formats are digital, as is the website.

So unless the Director accepts cassettes in analog (and will explain how they are to be submitted and will later convert them digitally), this format is too antiquated (and will continue to be even more so) for use in a program that proposes to extend decades and centuries into the future.

If, however, analog audio cassettes are acceptable, they must be sent as a complete unit, edited (or raw), ready for conversion and inclusion as is.

How does this then appear at the website?

It will be one more exciting way to be able to permanently hear what your kid or your cousin said. The spoken words will come from a computer speaker, assuming the computer has voice software.

If each member records various times during his life about topics that other family members want to hear, those will be posted on the website. You may be able to hear your great-grandmother tell of her dreams and realities when she was 15 or 25, as she recalls them.

But if your living family tree starts now and you are 15, everyone in the family from here on will be able to hear your thoughts at that age. And you will too even when you are 45 or 65.

Is that important? It's almost unbelievable. This potential has only become available and affordable to most of the populace in the past decade. In a very real sense, all who participate in sharing sound recordings are true pioneers surfing on the auditory cutting edge!

The written word has been around many thousands of years, and that's a good way to read what kin thought—or at least what they wrote. It works best for the educated and literate, but excludes a lot of otherwise interesting and worthy souls.

Photos have been around about 150 years to tell us what relatives looked like, at least at the moment the photo was shot. And portrait paintings for the rich extend our visual understanding far earlier.

But nobody alive has heard Abraham Lincoln speak. His later family is unaware that he had a high, reedy voice that broke with emotion. And while Uncle Chester doesn't carry the clout of Old Abe, he is alive but his grandchildren may well be equally as deprived if he won't take 15 or 20 minutes and talk a bit on some electronic sound capturing device and let the Director put those tones on a quickly attainable website so his family can share a touch of his oral soul when they wish. We're close to fiddling with immortality here.

Video

Imagine what a contemporary of Shakespeare, even better Julius Caesar, would make of our technological wonders today! Words and writing they knew, and history was in full flow even then, but capturing an exact likeness (and making faithful copies) of another person by using a little box? Come on. Then being able to ensnare another's voice as well, carry it around in a littler box, and reproduce it at whim?

Why not make atoms dance on a pin?

Where is the world headed? Maybe to let us have that person move around and talk, and capture both at once, hide it inside a different box, plug that box into another box, and send the whole show—forms, motion, and noise, even order and purpose, in its original color and tone—by wire (why not just do it through the air?) to a cousin across the ocean who, with another box, could see it all as if it were being immediately performed on command. (Oh yes, she can even call in her cousins and they can all see it again and again, until she is hanged as a witch—one hopes not on a family tree—or until everybody else can perform the same magic.)

Isn't that video?

This chapter will be short. What sane people never imagined is now commonplace. Juice up a digital hand-held video camera, insert a digital video cassette, turn on the record button, and fire away.

The point is that you can photo your kids with their kids opening Christmas gifts and blasting new vaporizers and monster guns, complete with shrieks and fake blood. Whether you hide that in a box or ship it off to unsuspecting friends, those moments of six or eight family members in action together are captured forever.

What is more extraordinary, if they are saved on the website, they are also alive to every family member for all time. It's not exactly a "JFK plays football with the family" documentary but it will mean even more to your grandkids' grandkids, one hopes.

It's all logistics and protocol here

By this time it has become obvious that a Family Board or a wise Director will need to set parameters on the items to be displayed at your living family tree website, and even what's included in the archives.

Why? Because everything sent takes time to receive, edit, and post, and because some things (like audio and video, particularly) take up lots of digital space and the family (or a rich familial benefactor) is paying for that space.

So the questions become:

- What kind of videos will be received? (One Christmas video of the entire family is probably much appreciated. Three decades of the same 30-minute extravaganza is probably 28 or 29 too many, although keeping them all in the personal family archives is a great idea.)
- How many videos per family?
- How long can they be? (Two-day cricket matches are less eagerly anticipated than ten-minute appointment videos of you and your family at your Supreme Court installation.)
- Are there technical or transmission requirements? (If the Director can't get the gem accepted by the website server, that says it all for at least a while. But do keep it yourself in case that changes.)

Then there is the issue of how you get the family follies out of the camera, into the computer, and to the Director in a form that can be readily adapted or viewed. Because video is space intensive, that means time intensive as well. So the Director will have to explain how the videos must be sent—the protocol.

So, rather than giving universal steps for downloading video here, follow (1) the instructions included with your video camera (since these vary considerably by camera) to get the contents downloaded on your computer, and/or (2) an explanation from the Director as to what is wanted and how it can be received for website display.

When family history comes full circle...

Could history, so fascinating to Shakespeare and Julius Caesar, bring us all back full fold? Like them, might we just gather the whole living clan together, in full flesh, to hug, laugh, tell stories, and share genes? Something like a living family reunion?

Members could now gather from far greater distances, cheaper, much quicker, and with far greater safety. And they could all use their own boxes to confiscate the others' likenesses, sounds, and movements, to store or send to even more kin.

Still, it might make much more sense to pool those images and their ideas and stories, send them to one person (bless the Director), and let that person, and successors for centuries, gather all of those images from every family member and make them instantly accessible to every other, by wire forever—or a thousand years, whichever comes last.

That sounds like a real living family tree to me.

Artefacts

A person can live almost as fully years or centuries later through the things they created, saved, built, or even rebuilt as they can in word or in film.

In fact, those to whom writing, music, or sound are difficult or where they don't excel may leave a misleading impression when their best embodiment is through the things they created or built.

So we add that dimension to the Living Family Tree, another way to leave things important from that family member to all those to follow.

Let's touch this topic later, in the Appendix, where the artefacts might most likely be seen, in Family Treasures in Print, the Family Treasure Box, perhaps Scrapbooks, and surely Other Attachments.

The best example of this was the mother of a teaching friend I knew whose grandmother passed days before she was born, but not before finishing a quilt and knitting a small baby blanket just for her.

The grandparents had lived in the roughest parts of Montana, nobody before her mother ever had a photo taken or could read more than their name, and those two items were the sum total of what she ever saw or could feel of her grandmother. They were kept in a special locked drawer. Just the kind of keepsake to be handed down and identified and shared in a Living Family Tree nearly forever.

Section 4

The Director

What we've read so far describes one of many ways your living family tree might look. It must reflect what your family wants preserved and shared and how they want that done.

Of course, once a plan is designed and in process, the family members must then accept and energetically support that design or plan and supply their own personal information to get the project launched and sustained.

Most important, though, is that somebody must be at the helm creating and initially directing the whole thing, and later a process must be designed to keep its leadership vital far into the future..

So let's find a leader who will get this extraordinary treasure up and running!

Finding that heroic first seed planter

Why not you? It goes without saying that you are clever—after all, you are reading this book!

And since you've continued reading this far, something about the idea is ringing your bell.

May I whisper a secret just to you before you start laughing or you flee. (If others are watching, just shield this page.) If you pull it off, if you get your own family's living tree up and growing, there is a HUGE REWARD that will be yours only, and almost forever. You will be the genius, a family hero for 200 or 500 years. You will be the mastermind, the legend, who had the tenacity, foresight, and skills to launch this family treasure! "No way!" you say, "Not me." And you list 137 reasons why you don't deserve accolades or could never be a hero.

Okay, but think again before you hand this book to another because FAMILY HERO or FAMILY LEGEND badges are real hard to get!

Yes, it will take work and time, but surely less time than most of us otherwise just waste. It will require days (scattered out) to get the frame set up, then probably some hours one night a week to tune it up, keep it running, and add a bit more substance each year.

Skill? Mostly it needs attention to detail; no genius stuff. (Soon enough a *Director's Guidebook* will be available that will do most of the work for you, with templates and submission guidelines, plus step-by-step instructions. Keep your eyes on our website: www.yourlivingfamilytree.com.)

Special preparation? Nothing you can't quickly learn, then perfect in the coming years. Since the foundation of the project is digital, you'll have to know how to use a computer, and be willing to learn some modifications as upgrades happen. Can you send and receive an email? Create a file? Save a photo as a .jpeg? You're almost there!

Think of a living family tree as a garden. Digging up the ground is a giant pain, but once it's done, the edible returns are worth far more than the odd hours spent planting and weeding. The best part? In this millennium, super new tools appear weekly that will do almost all of your digging!

Keeping the tree growing straight and tall almost forever

Let's call the tree (and website) keeper the Director. Whether that is you, you and another family member, or some other hero-to-be, the most important thing that you should know is that this project can be 100 good to great things for folks carrying your genes for many, many years to come.

Starting it is the single most important step. The second most important is tending the tree so that it blooms and grows straight and tall almost forever. (Lots of future Directors will help make that happen. More on that in the next chapter.)

A heretical thought also suggests itself once the tree is firmly rooted: the family could even hire outsiders to do the collection and keep the project thriving.

But at the outset, its creator should be an insider, a trusted family member to get the first flame lit and bring their kin to it.

Let's ask some starter questions while you mull over becoming the one-ever-in-the-family first Director:

- What kind of equipment would you need?
- Would a Family Board help?
- What about a family reunion?
- How could I keep the family involved?
- Which members do I approach first?
- Isn't money involved somewhere?
- What do I do in what order?

Equipment needed

In a nutshell, your living family tree will grow by bits and bytes. It's really gene-bound humans shared by electronics, so while the Director needs the most equipment and software at the outset, that's not much more, as we said, than what a PC or Mac, even a laptop, today already provides.

The family members need to access the Internet, to email, and to occasionally add attachments. If they have a digital and/or a video camera, all the better, but the family can pool there or the Director might loan them out as needed.

What do you do about the retrograde uncle on your tree who rabidly opposes computers and vows never to foul his fingers on any keyboard? Love him nonetheless, and work with and around him. Mail him a printed copy of the files once a year; have his kids send in any forms or information that he will share, take photos of him at the reunion, get him in the group video, and thank God that he is still healthy and feisty.

Within this generation almost all families will have a computer accessible, at home, work, church, library, or somewhere. And it will become an even more integral part of every home and education in the future.

Another aside—at some future point the issue won't be computer availability or the skill to use it (almost all will have both), it will be keeping up with the electronic changes as they happen—like pushing a key and having a semblance of the actual person appear on screen or emerge from it, able to converse and laugh and share memories or reflections through some holographic process linked to saved and artificial intelligence. But let's not scare you away with what might be.

To get your living family tree fully leafed, the Director will likely need some or all of these things, depending on your tree's spread:

- A family website, registered, and the requisite protocol software to post and make changes on it
- a computer with lots of memory (a PC XP or higher, or a current MAC, will have the best multimedia capacity)
- a server, a modem; and DSL (or some speed equivalent)

- a good scanner (mostly to convert the odd item submitted [some from that retrograde uncle]—like paper photos, maps, or printed matter—into storable and usable text, .jpeg , or .pdf format)
- CD/DVD software, discs, and labels (primarily to responsibly back up the digital LFT project and store it safely off computer in an usable format)
- A Family Treasure Box (probably just that in the beginning, a box with a lid kept in a dry, safe, clean place)
- family tree software (or at least a copy of the key files of the website as it develops)
- photo editing software (like PhotoShop or equivalent)
- perhaps audio editing software (like Adobe Audition or something less expensive)
- a digital camera with a USB link and related software
- a small digital voice recorder (with microphone and batteries), probably for family reunions or to loan to family members as requested
- a video camera and film units, discs, and storage software, most likely to use at or lend for family gatherings or reunions

The Director will have to know how to use the equipment and the software; link to the website; accept and store/convert items from the family; back it up when prudent; communicate with kin (and others), and keep it all in good repair and current enough to do the job.

A second major responsibility will be the preparation or customization and sharing of simple submission guidelines that explain to every family member how they should send the requested items so they are easily and quickly postable at the website.

Don't panic! Your living family tree won't have to be created full flush. It's much like that proverbial elephant—if you want to eat him, you must do it one bite at a time. The same with creating the tree: one byte at a time! And you needn't do it all alone. Nor must it be started in the next 20 minutes—though that's a great idea!

A Family Board?

Is a Family Board necessary? Not at all, at least not in the beginning, though the family may want a loose group of relatives gathered to see that the project keeps running, particularly during times of weak Directors or when it's necessary to change leadership or design.

We all know that the more cooks in the kitchen, the slower and poorer the stew.

Yet at two times there can be strength in numbers: in this case, at the outset and all the times since!

With something new like your living family tree the biggest initial problems are likely to be family buy-in, computer set-up assistance and expertise, and funding.

For family buy-in, selecting the most influential person in each family branch for a Family Board and getting their support and encouragement may go a long way to getting their kids' support, and so on up and down the line. But if you're a small family and the only branches are your own kids and they are still young, that wisdom might be 30 years premature.

The core couple should be on the Board too.

There might also be a pinch of good sense to putting the two family computer and website use wizards on the Board, as long as they are in full understanding and agreement that from the outset the Director is in charge of the living family tree design and implementation.

Having the digital bright lights helping from the beginning might also greatly alleviate initial funding concerns. In short, they might help create the website free, review the submission guidelines, and have better insight into the kind of equipment that is needed and where it can be found inexpensively—or less!

But do you need a Family Board to start or run your living family tree? Not if the initial Director just takes hold, creates a fun and easy-to-use website, and gets the family enthused and participating. Then, at the point that a new Director is required or outside advice is sensible, a Family Board might be formed. (In some families the project might just be passed down from the old Directors to the new ones forever. If the project works well and the family eagerly participates, the members probably don't care a whit about its selection or administration.)

If you do want or need a Family Board, keep it manageable in size (many recommend boards of 3-7), as local as possible to reduce the cost and time of travel (if that's important to the respective members), and fully informed as to its purpose. Then let it determine it own operating mechanism.

Some responsibilities of a Family Board might be the selection (or approval) of the Director, raising and overseeing operating funds, endorsing the general design of the living family tree, helping provide necessary tools that the Director needs but doesn't have, and giving the project its proper launching and blessing.

There may be some group decision-making too, as suggested elsewhere in the book, like where the Family Treasure Box is kept and what things don't "fit" in it (like every Little League uniform or every old doll) or what information is strictly family-accessible and what is shared with the world.

´One or many Family Reunions

The quickest way to launch your living family tree is for some hero to design it, set it up, and get it going while all along getting family input as it grows in size, stature, and desirability.

But a powerful counter argument says that nothing would launch an LFT project faster or keep it on track better than a family reunion.

Okay, some families are scattered to the seven corners of the earth (or is it eight?) and getting together would be a logistical and financial nightmare. (One alternative, grouping together and setting up interactive conference video calls, is already easy to do and surprisingly inexpensive.)

… And some families would be quickly reduced by murder if certain members even caught sight of other members! (In those families, maybe not every member is invited, or you'll want to wait until the most violent are in the slammer…)

… And every family, or just about, has someone in the ranks who is guaranteed to become an instant jerk, get bubbly drunk, or set anxieties skyrocketing. (So the Hollywood version of blissful blending has a few kinks…)

Any more objections?

The point stands that almost nothing can pull the branches of this kind of human tree closer together than when all gather to play badminton or Mexican Train dominoes, sing, watch old family movies, swim at the lake, and share stories in concert. Just getting the kids and grandkids together so they know each other, that alone is a familial investment that's hard to beat.

An ideal world would have a disciplined and reliable family member (Aunt Ruth? Brother Jesse? You've got to be kidding!) grasp the genius and worth of your living family tree idea, propose setting it up to serve your family for the next thousand years, and put the whole thing in motion.

That person might initially invite two or three close family members for a meal to discuss the idea. Assuming the project was embraced (however madly), from that gathering might come a Family Board, and from that Board the initiator would gladly be proclaimed the first Director.

The Family Board might then request that the family have a reunion some months hence—sometimes busy families need a year of anticipation so the dates can get saved and protected on everyone's calendar.

The question then becomes whether the Board and Director spring the project fully formed on the unsuspecting reunion revellers (who think they are gathering to canoe down the river and drink beer) or create the framework first, then explain (mostly through e- and snail mail) what it's all about, why it's the greatest idea since sex, and roughly what it asks of each family member, followed by the reunion at which it will be discussed and dissected in greater depth—and approved.

What else might they do at that reunion? Perhaps renew (or create) bonds, make some collective and individual audio CDs, and see who wants to organize an Ancestral Family Tree as part of the same, extended project? (Attendees will also get a chance to heft grandpa's M1 from the War, marvel at Aunt Belle's six prize-winning quilts, and carefully taste Bachelor Billy's canned quince jam.)

Also, taking group pictures of the pioneer family members of the new living family tree will be a popular attraction. (To prove that those in the photos aren't cardboard, interactive videos of the earliest generations might also be shot!)

Actually, much more (yet much less evident) is afoot at family reunions. Roots grow and memories form that last the participants' lifetimes, with benefits lasting many generations longer. It starts with the Jones branch challenging the Curtis group in volleyball, or with the kids under 18 taking on the fogies in softball, bingo, or canoe races. It's where four-person teams, as mixed as possible, collectively head out on a treasure-scavenger hunt, or where clusters play Charades, Sequence, or cards. Where the rest talk and frolic and "be" while the kids pose and flirt and race to the pine tree.

So there's more to family reunions than launching your living family tree, but it's hard to imagine a more significant gathering or one with a greater potentially unifying, century-binding effect than that reunion where the LFT idea and its enabling protocols are introduced, defined, approved, and set in action.

How that reunion is organized and that presentation is made is entirely up to you. That's the miracle of leadership, and the person taking up this mantle is a leader.

Conversely, if one simply ignores that potentially magical union of a LFT and a reunion, or something like it once they know it is possible, then much, much more might be lost than the games and tag and the tale-telling of today. In a growingly atomistic world, any opportunity to weave a genetic web of love, acceptance, support, and joy like a living family tree (and all that can come from it), and to give it growing bones and participatory nutrients to last for centuries, is a singular chance just waiting for a leader (and dedicated support cadre) to make happen. A family reunion may indeed be an integral, history-making step in that process.

Still, introducing the idea and setting it to flow at a family reunion may just not work. If not, then do it the old-fashioned way: by mail, e-mail, in person, and by CD. Getting the living family tree planted, now and firmly, is what really counts.

Getting the whole family involved

How is that done? Probably by one person seeing the worth and joy of the idea and convincing their kin that they need a living family tree, or by their stepping up and initiating the website and completing some key links to get the concept in motion, or a combination of both.

Sending family members a copy of this book (bolstered by raging words of enthusiasm) might help.

A family reunion, as just mentioned, may well be the pivotal point where all see the light.

Whichever path you follow, your living family tree's creation and the individual members' participation usually take place at three stages: (1) somebody embraces the idea and gets the core structure up and going, (2) the rest of the family joins in by sharing their information, and (3) it perpetuates itself into the future, with coming generations taking the leadership and individually contributing.

Nothing is more important than the creation of a vibrant, easy-to-use, accurate, well-administered website that draws the family members closer to those with whom they share a unique bond. Once that happens, involvement becomes "the" thing to do, a kind of pleasant family obligation like attending picnics, visiting kin, and going to the graduations and marriages.

But there is a time factor. The more one waits to start, the greater the chance that some immediate member will no longer be among the living.

Focussing on the oldest and youngest first

All things aren't equal when your living family tree is being planted. Age, for example.

With a regular family tree it doesn't much matter which root you tap first. In truth, Great-uncle Hester is just as dead today as he will be next Tuesday and in no greater hurry in either case to have his birth date recorded.

But the whole idea of capturing a person's soul (in a sort of physical way; at least some of their living memories, words, laughter, and on-the-spot wisdom) while their heart still beats does hint at a ticking clock. So, in a quest to seize singularity while it is seizable, those with the longest time cards must move to the top of the list.

As must new tykes when they enter your family and the world, since that must be captured at or around the moment.

If there's a sensible time priority, then, consider beginning with the ends and moving quickly to the center. Every family member counts, all are important, but some really are more important than others right now.

For those on the older end of the mortal continuum, getting them involved may take extra energy and time, too.

There's the latest "Personal Information Sheet" to complete, plus as much of the basic information for as many of the earlier, missed sheets as possible. There may be photos from earlier years to sort through and have converted into digital format, plus a contemporary digital shot or several. Why not a recorded interview with the Director or a close member on digital audio, to save as an audio CD? Video shots of the person doing active things (like walking, gardening, lawn bowling, or playing with the grandkids) are great additions to the collection too.

Are memoirs out of the question? What about some Family Treasure Box keepsakes, plus some treasures in print, like early family letters from their grandparents, artwork, their citizenship papers, or a poem they wrote?

Because the oldest family members probably aren't wired or computer-savvy, here's where their closest kin can be of huge assistance, to help them get this done quickly and thoroughly.

The newest members are much easier. What you really need about them comes from their parents: the birth information and a photo (or many) so you can share an immediate "Tip of the Hat" Acclamation, then get them into the Family Directory and the Key Date List. The next time they check in is at five!

The rest of the family members are still untapped mines, to wend their way into the tree with less alacrity but no less importance. Yet, it's hard to imagine that if their grandparents and their youngest kids, or brother or sister, are on file and part of this new living family tree, they won't get the bug and want to be included too. (The alternative is to be eternally bugged, or so it will seem, by the pesky Director.)

Oh yes, there's that equally pesky business of money.

Money and bill paying

Sometimes the family lucks out. An eager, savvy member has all of the digital equipment (or scrounges up what they don't have from their kids, friends, or some computer graveyard) *and* either knows how to use it or will quickly learn. Bingo!

If it were always that easy—and if that paid all the bills. So the family project probably needs a family project kitty. It's unfair to expect one person to singly build, then row a boat for an entire brood—or pay their bills.

Early on, then, in the set-up plans the Director and the family should determine the costs, where the needed money will come from, and who will see to the process.

The most obvious costs are computer-related.

The Director, who runs the program on a daily basis, needs a computer and appropriate website software. They will need a modem, a scanner, CD/DVD software and discs, and perhaps photo-editing and audio-editing software—if not right away, soon enough. So any of those items that the Director doesn't have must be provided or bought. (A few cables and USB connections work wonders too.)

In addition, there will be the website costs, a bit of the phone bill, some overhead, and occasional phone calls to inquiring family members.

I'm presuming that there will be no salary for the Director (yes, the labor truly is a thing of love), but if the family can find a deep pocket or two, that might also be in the realm of funding consideration.

How much money are we talking about? Maybe several hundred dollars a year. The more complex the LFT is, the higher the costs, particularly if labor is being paid. Most of the money will initially go into website creation and rental, plus some mailing and phone calls to the unlinked.

How will the finances be handled, and by whom?

Almost every family includes some trustworthy soul who enjoys and is adept at coffer control. You've found the treasurer! However the funds are gathered, this person deposits them in a separate bank account and, at set times, pays the Director for the bills rendered.

And if you don't have a Family Board but you're eager to get started? It's still best to separate the directorship from the money. So ask the person in your family that you and the others most trust to assume this wee responsibility, and then get on with the more important task of getting your living family tree up and running.

Where the money will come from is the most difficult question. Asking some of the family members to kick into a kitty for a project that doesn't exist is likely to alienate them to the point that they won't participate.

In an ideal world two suggestions pop up.

One, the Director foots the bill until the website is up, the project is visible, its benefits are evident, and the subject of financing it can later be discussed at a family reunion or through a Family Board. Alas, the cruelty is that the Director must risk that the family won't pay the accumulated costs or bills.

A brighter prospect is that one of the more affluent family members would provide a starter endowment to get the project up and running for its first year, during which a process could be created to accept other voluntary family endowments or contributions for future maintenance. If the living family tree were to be established as a non-profit entity (with contributions tax-deductible), that might provide an additional incentive to contribute, and a requisite way to handle future costs and fund management. Who knows, it might even become a font from which scholarships, grants, and repayable loans for family members might emanate.

You're ready! What do you do right now?

Enough already! You're frothing with anticipation. How do you begin?

Here's 10 steps, perhaps in this order, that seem to be the most logical. But it's your project, your time, probably your bucks at the outset, and your energy, so mix and match as you wish:

1. Check the Internet to see if you can get a website with your family name in it, preferably to hide at .com (since most people automatically use that suffix). If your surname is Happy, see if "happy.com" is available. Or you might consider "happyfamily.com" or "happylivingfamilytree.com." Avoid site names with hyphens.

2. If you can find a good URL (site name) that is easy to remember for all your kin now and later, you should register it before somebody else does!

3. Visit www.yourlivingfamilytree.com to see if there is ready-to-use software available to more quickly set up your living family tree.

4. Decide the minimum number of starter items you want to develop at your website in the first year, and what you will ask family members to prepare and submit at the outset so there will be enough interesting things to see and share. Then

think forward for five years and create a vision of how the full website will look at that time, itemizing which new sections you will add (and the family will be asked to complete and submit) during each of those five successive years. That will be your living family tree master plan!

5. Once you have a vision of your living family tree and you know what must be done to implement it for the next five years, contact a couple (or many) family members, explain what you want to start, and ask for their response, help, suggestions, or specific assistance. Mostly ask: if you take the leadership, will they join in—and help generate participation and buy-in from their family and kids, so your family history from its members during their lifetimes can be preserved for now and for generations to come?

6. If they are rabid with excitement and passionately eager to get started, ask if they think a Family Board would be useful or needed to help you get the new project started and smoothly functioning. If they say yes, enlist them right then, and request that one of them take the lead and get such a Family Board formed. (To let the Board find its own legs, it's best to let others take the initiative in its formation.)

7. In the meantime, get the content rolling by preparing your own information for the first sections or links that you will create. If, for example, you decide to start with a current age Personal Information Sheet, the Family Directory, and photos in the first year, decide what you would like from each family member, then provide that information about yourself. That will make visible at least one sample page (or several) for each category that you can place at the website to guide others as they prepare their submissions.

8. At the same time, for each of the sections you begin with, consult the sample Family Submission Guides to see if they need modification or customization for your particular family. For example, you might initially use the Personal Information Sheets at ages 5, 15, 25, 45, and 65. Do you want to

change them to better reflect your own family situation and interests? If so, create new Family Submission Guides, then ask your family members to pick the sheet closest to their present age (so you don't have to wait 15 years for them to get involved!), put their current age in the title, and fill it in. Then you do the same. If you are 32, look at the Age 25 Sheet and add appropriate information to expand it to a person 32 (the subsequent age sheet will offer hints). Your completed sheet will be the example they will likely see first on the website.

9. Do the same with the Family Directory and the photos that you want on the family website. Perhaps list all of the family members and ask them to provide the current address and contact information. Tell them the kind, number, and size photos you would gladly add to the person's information sheet, and how you want those sent too. To show them what you mean, you must get the same kind of photos of yourself and place them on the website as examples.

10. Is a family reunion appropriate to launch this new project? If so, you may wish to have a website ready to go but wait until the family gathers to unveil it all at once. You could suggest to the Family Board that its grand first task might be to convene the family reunion! (Or just snag another family member or two to help you get your genetic vagabonds together for a fun surprise.)

You get the idea. Some families will demand that you display extraordinary ingenuity and flexibility before they will even look at such an odd project as a living family tree. Other families will shriek (politely) with delight and dig right in. Some won't even be that polite.

Most families will probably do a little of all: ignore, nod, applaud, and/or yelp with gusto.

What do you do when not many yelp? Go ahead anyway, create a dandy website, gather what's offered by the brighter and more giving members, try to lovingly squeeze what you can from the meanest, and get the kids and the elders on the 1000-year bandwagon as quickly as possible.

Just keep thinking of your grandchildren's grandchildren tapping a computer key (or will they just say a word and the images will appear on a nearby wall?) and all of their family since well before the oldest living member was born will appear, in word and photo and flesh, to share their earlier lives, dreams, accomplishments, and life story—all because you were motivated and wise enough to get the whole living history collection up and going! This is how to be a 100- or 1,000-year hero to kin you will never know.

Now and the Future

When you're talking about starting a new project, even one with a thousand years (or legs), the now and the future are both the same. And when the project is put together from whole cloth, from "what if" and "why can't we?", the now is pretty much when you declare that it has begun—like when a family website exists and there's something on it—and the future is from that point forward.

Everything you do with your living family tree is unique because none of your friends (even the smartest ones) actually have one as this book is written. I am simply offering suggestions, verbal ideas with loosely-drawn examples, but how those actually look in practice and how creatively you can improve upon them is in your hands.

Welcome to a grand—and very exciting—new world!

If somebody doesn't plant this tree now...

The world will not end, any more than it did yesterday without such a tree in bloom! On the surface it seems that there's no urgency at all to get this project up and in final form.

Even if one sets a leisurely goal of three or six months to get a website established and initially populated with a couple of key web pages, and then the deadline is missed by a few months more, probably nothing catastrophic will occur.

Except on the long shot that Cousin Bob might just stop breathing in the prime of his life for no discoverable reason, leaving tragically before the living family tree arrives. So there will be is no oral interview with Bob, we will have no idea what his dreams were or what he was proudest of, and we can't see him at the dinner table in the reunion video.

"That's sad," you say, "but not irreparable. I knew Bob despite his not being on record, audio, or video." But his grandkids may not have, and it's certain that in 2100 nobody in your direct family would know much more about him than that he existed. He'd be listed on your living family tree, but a large part of what future family members might have shared with him won't be.

So if nobody plants the tree at all, you and all your direct relatives and all their get will miss out on the many benefits of being remembered, admired, respected, learned from, and modelled after for a long, long, long time.

Somebody has to put the seed in the ground and add some water or this tree won't grow.

(Don't despair or hide in the attic. Most of the readers of this book will be in the same sad pickle: they won't do anything either.)

Yet if you do get a living family tree organized and running but don't do it right now, whatever that means, at least you did it (or found a relative to do it), and that's a huge feather in your cap. The delay just means that Uncle Bob probably got left out if the thing dawdled too long…

If, on the other hand, you create a living family tree, it gets going soon, and the oldest and at least Uncle Bob are quickly added, think of the legacy you have created: the full train on track and everybody aboard. Yours will be a name to be remembered, you're the family hero, and all that stuff, 200 or 500 or 1000 years from now. Or did I say that before?

Keeping it going far into the future...

There are two key reasons to create and continually maintain your living family tree—and improve it as new tools appear in the future:

- For current use by your living family now, and
- For retrospective use about and by the entire family at any time from then back to your tree's creation (and further back if it also includes an "Ancestral Family Tree")

Assuming that the program gets started, much of the future success of your living family tree will depend upon the quality of its directorship. An effective Director will keep the family involved and enthusiastically participating. But how does the family keep selecting fervent, capable directors far into the future? Some ways that continuity might be assured:

- A Family Board, itself changed annually or at a set number of years, chooses the Director
- Each Director chooses his or her successor
- The Director is paid an honorable fee to perform the duties quickly and responsibly
- The LFT is divided into several directorships, each responsible for specific categories
- The direction is hired out to a person or firm that professionally directs living family trees, under the broader supervisory guidance of the Family Board
- A Family Foundation replaces the Family Board and is in charge of the selection and supervision of the LFT Director

- Some combination of the above

Surely as important as the selection process of a Director will be the perceived worth of the living family tree in keeping it vital and fresh through the centuries. If indeed it binds family members together; creates a spirit of genetic union and pride; displays true-life, almost three-dimensional models and examples that in turn display the potential that each member shares, and affords every member an honest historical seat at the family table (a sort of in-house immortality that proves they lived and tried), it's hard to imagine that the honor of directing such an entity wouldn't be much sought by those within the family, particularly after its existence has become a worthy, comfortable tradition.

And if it disappears for a while?

Such a gloomy thought since it has yet to appear at all! Worse yet, that it would do so because the family itself ceases to exist...

Let's shake this murky mantle by accepting the fact that any living family tree might suffer short periods of inactivity, but that it's even more likely to continue marching proudly intact for hundreds (even many, many hundreds) of years.

There are two fixes to inactivity. One is to make it active again, with as much repair as possible made to the parched tree to bring it back to full form, filling in the periods and people who were missed or incompletely included.

The other is to accept a tree that can't be made to grow, but to preserve that which was begun in as many historical repositories as possible. The website might be maintained as a frozen catalog of kin of the past, or it might be saved on CDs, DVDs, or the best measure at the time and distributed to all the members of the family then living.

Later, should an inspired family member wish to restore the living family tree, that which was gathered earlier can be included—or built from.

Even if your LFT only existed for a short period of time, a few years or decades, those involved with it reaped the benefits it was designed to share while it was around.

Your living family tree in
200, 500, or 1,000 years?

It's hard to imagine what life will even be like in 500 or 1,000 years, though if the past is a guide most people will still be doing the same types of life-enriching and –sustaining things they are doing right now.

Family will surely be a continually cohesive force (temporarily setting aside those rebellious teen years that make even the mention of anything "family" faintly toxic). There will be curiosity about where one comes from, what earlier family members were like, what made them do what they did, what were the consequences of their acts, who dreamed large and saw their dreams come true…

The means of sharing the information will be different, as much so as parchment has yielded to print and that to the digital ethers.

When I was young there was no television; typewriters were clunky and rare; long-distance telephone calls were expensive and full of static (if they could be made at all); anybody 60 years old was in fact very old, and if one was lucky they knew their grandparents for a few years before they passed away.

Only as the twenty-first century unfolds does a living family tree make much sense. So it is hard to imagine at the cusp of the new possibility, of preserving ourselves and our living relatives multi-dimensionally forever, how many more changes are in store even in our own lifetime, much less that of our grandchildren, and theirs.

All of which begs the question that this book asks: Just because at last we can create and maintain a living family tree, should we?

The answer is yes.

And today is the very day to get it started.

Appendix

The whole idea of "your living family tree" is probably mind boggling at the first reading. It makes sense and it seems possible, but it's like getting a huge jigsaw puzzle to assemble without any picture to guide you. How and where do you start putting it together?

This Appendix might help. It's a menu of 17 possible sections of the tree, in as plain a format as possible, to suggest one structure that the described parts might assume. Each is a starting block that invites you, and your family, to build from it, to make it better, more complete, prettier, quicker, and to give it even more meaning and relevance.

Select three or five of these choices, or seeds, and grow your living family tree from them. They are word based. Add in the other "ways"—the photos, sound, and motion—when you wish. The idea is to create a core structure, to get the tree growing quickly so you and your living kin get recorded while your mind is fresh and you're still in the pink. The rest is 1000 minor adjustments!

Personal Information Repository

Of all the sections in this chapter surely none is as central and important as a Personal Information Repository.

The challenge the repository poses is determining what you want to gather for the ages, how it is best collected, and how you want it submitted by your family members.

There is also the delicate balance of asking the family members to share as much as they wish but not requesting so much at any one time that few or nobody will respond.

Finally, how do you handle the editing?

It sounds so easy: "Just tell us about yourself and we will post it for a thousand years."

But any part of that may scare or anger some of your kin. "It's none of your business," is a common enough dismissal.

Others will so cleanse their description of their otherwise quite human, slightly sin-tinged life that future readers will wonder how they escaped beatification!

Oh well, your living family tree needs roots. You must start somewhere. You need their facts, and facts are the best roots of all.

What should you gather for the ages?

At least basic information, plus ample opportunities for later elaboration or additional sharing.

Since facts change as people grow, it's best to break this up into age plateaus, and remind the participants every five years, say, what is on their "Personal Information Repository" page(s) so they can update the data while the details are at hand.

When should the information be gathered?

The first fact gathering might be shortly after birth.

The second might be at five years of age, or about the time that tykes enter kindergarten.

Perhaps 15 might be a fun check-in. The boy or girl is at long last literate and able to add impressions and dreams to the cold or at least second-hand data already posted by their mother or father.

Then maybe at 25, 40, and 65. (Or marriage, when the last kid graduates from high school, and when the person collects Social Security, or its equivalent.)

(Friends had other ideas about the logical times. One felt that it should be more often during the participants' youth, suggesting 13, 16, 21, and 25. Another liked conception points, or as the person enters high school, college, the work world, and retirement.)

Too often? Too regimented? Then make it as informal or irregular as you wish. Inviting any family member to create and add to his or her own page(s) at any time would surely be the least structured, but would anybody actually do it without some age or activity reminder? The greatest fear is that sharing first-hand knowledge about the touch points of one's life will be postponed until well past their death, leaving it in the hands of others to guess at the facts lest the procrastinator slip totally out of mind and existence.

Should the Information be accessible to the public?

We asked this before. It's your choice. There is a lot of private information posted at the Personal Information Repository so prudence might suggest that each person's files be under wraps (available only to family members) during that person's lifetime. Then at the person's death, as some of it is used on the "In Memoriam" page, it becomes openly accessible. There's no longer a reason for the privacy, (Or perhaps the family policy will be to keep it closed for 25 years, or even 100 years after death. If it's never open for others, though, it defeats the purpose of sharing with future family.)

What information is best gathered when?

You have to start somewhere, so why don't we offer some lists of basic data and observations that might be appropriate at the six suggestion time plateaus, with the recommendation that you modify these as you wish to better meet your family's needs, your cultural mores or expectations, and the grander vision you have of your living family tree.

Personal Information at Birth, *prepared by parent or other*

Complete name of baby (first, middle, last):
Origin(s) of baby's name(s):
The baby's ethnicity:
Date of birth:
Time of birth:
Length (height) at birth:
Weight at birth:
Where born? (hospital/home, location, state, country):
Delivering doctor's name:

Family in attendance at birth:
Godparents (name[s], address[es]):
Where the parents lived at time of birth:
Name/age of mother at the baby's birth:
Name/age of father at the baby's birth:
Living grandparents (with age, location of residence)
Describe where and when labor first began:

How did the mother get to the hospital?

Any health issues?

Was the baby born with hair? (Color?)
Teeth? (Number?)

Other observations about the baby's birth or earliest days?

Mother:

Father:

At the age of 5 (or entering kindergarten), *prepared by
parent or other*

Preschools attended (if any)/age at each:
Kindergarten to attend (with location/state):
Address of family residence:
Other brothers/sisters in family (with ages):
Height (date):
Weight (date):
Color of hair:
Color of eyes:
Number of teeth:
Favorite sports:

Favorite activities:

Favorite TV shows?

Know the alphabet?
Count to 50?
Read full sentences?
Carry a tune?

Other observations about your five-year-old child?

Mother:

Father:

Asked to the child; response recorded by parent or other: "If I had to describe you to another (boy/girl) your age, what would I say?"

[Age five is a great time to supplement this information repository with a video (or audio) of the child, with questions asked that appropriate to that age, plus, on video, some action tape of the child playing and interacting with siblings and parents.]

At the age of 15 (or entering high school), *prepared by the person*

(Add any additional comments you wish after each category.)

Schools attended after kindergarten (grades, locations of each school):
Grade school teachers before high school:
Favorite teachers (with reasons):
Sports played (teams, position[s], years, championships, awards):
Favorite sports teams:
Do/can you cycle five miles?
Do/can you swim?

Do/can you cook a full meal?

Do/can you speak a foreign language? (Which?)

I can also _____ (Add other abilities.)

Musical activities (instruments played, groups sung or played with, years):

Favorite musical stars or groups:

Other activities (details about each, years, awards):

Five favorite friends about your age right now:

States or countries you have visited (years):

Baptized (date, location, pastor's name):

What do you want to do when you are fully grown up?

What job or position would you most want to have when you're an adult?

Which adults outside your family do you most admire?

What's the dumbest thing a person your age could do?

If a long-lost uncle wanted to know what you are like, how would you describe yourself right now?

What is the prettiest place you have ever visited? (Why?)

The best books you have read so far:

Your three favorite TV shows:

Your three favorite CDs or DVDs:

Describe your mother:

Describe your father:

Describe your grandparents (with their age, if living):

List any health changes or updates (this knowledge could be important to your children or future relatives).

What specific health challenges are you facing:

What medications or treatments are you taking?

What is the prognosis, and how has the ailment or condition progressed?

Who is your current doctor for those treatments?

An open question—"What is the most significant contribution you have made to the world during this time period (or so far), and what's the next contribution you intend to make?"

Why not start a life list now (that you can modify, check off, or add to at any time in the future) of things you absolutely want to do, see, experience, share, or start during your lifetime?

Anything else you would like to share at 15?

At age 25 (or _____), or at the time of your marriage:

(Add any additional comments you wish after each category. Can you provide digital photos of the key events or people of this time period to augment or help illustrate your accounts?)

If you have a spouse, name of the person and how you met:
Age of both of you at marriage:
Where the marriage took place, the date, and, if in a
    church, the church, location, and name of clergy:
Best man:
Maid of honor:
Names of those in bridal party:
Your family members in attendance, with age of each then:
Spouse's family members in attendance, with age of each
    then:
Other things the family should know about the marriage:

Schools you have attended since you last listed your per-
    sonal information:
Favorite teachers in high school (with reasons):
Awards or achievements during your high school days:
Easiest and most difficult subjects in high school:
Fondest memories of high school:

Dumbest thing you did in high school:

What you would do differently if you had to repeat your high school years:

Your highest job aspiration when you graduated from high school:

ACT, SAT, other test scores for college or graduate school:

Colleges or universities attended (with number of months and location of each school):

Academic majors (and minors) at each college:

Degrees received, by institution, with date of receipt:

What you liked best and least about each institution:

Most interesting academic thing you did each year:

Most interesting non-academic thing you did each year:

Name and information about your top heart throb each year (or semester) at college:

Jobs you held, with a description of the responsibilities, during college:

College-related activities you participated in, with dates and positions held:

Other things the family should know about your college time:

List all of the vehicles you have owned since you received a driver's license:

The date you took possession, the cost of each, and its ultimate disposition:

Sports or activities in which you have participated during and since high school, with details about each:

Favorite coaches (with reasons):

Outside of college, list all the jobs you have held since high school, and the primary responsibilities of each:

List the positions you have held (with dates) in your primary vocation(s):

List vocationally-related certifications or training-related awards (with date):

Favorite bosses (with reasons):

Location and description of each residence after high school (excluding college):

Name and information about your top heart throb(s) before or after college:

Military service (branch, ranks attained, achievement awards, honors, locations served at, type of activities, other information):

Particular friends made in service, description, details:

Pets you have had or cared for: name, kind of animal, gender, years:

Giving your druthers, of any job which one would you most want in your life:

A description of your spiritual life or vocation, please, including beliefs and actions:

Your participation in organized religion: church(es), location(s), pastors:

List any health changes or updates (this knowledge could be important to your children or future relatives).

What specific health challenges are you facing:

What medications or treatments are you taking?

What is the prognosis, and how has the ailment or condition progressed?

Who is your current doctor for those treatments?

An open question—"What is the most significant contribution you have made to the world during this time period (or so far), and what's the next contribution you intend to make?"

A quick summary of the past decade, please:
Remember that life list you started at 15 (or later) of things you absolutely want(ed) to do, see, experience, share, or start during your lifetime? Why not modify it, check things off, or add new items to it now?

Anything else you would like to share at 25 (or ___)?

At age 45 (or ___), or when your last child graduates from high school:

(Add any additional comments you wish after each category. Can you provide digital photos of the key events or people of this time period to augment or help illustrate your accounts?)

Describe your kids, in order please: name, gender, age now, where they are educationally or vocationally, a sentence or two describing each:
If any were adopted or were from different fathers or mothers, better clarify that too:
City in which each child was born:
Your children now married, with name of spouse, date of marriage, place:
Grandchildren you have now—names, ages, parents:

Since your information posting at 25, where you have lived: addresses, cities, states:
Homes you have owned, with location, year purchased, (price):

New pets since 25 :

What jobs you and your spouse have had since you were married—positions and companies:
Favorite jobs (and why):

How high you expect to climb in the vocational field, and
 by what date:
Singular vocational contributions you have made:
What else we should know about you vocationally:

Since 25, places you and your family have traveled together:

Organizations or associations you have taken part in since
 25, with offices held:
If not well known, what those groups do:
Civic elected offices you have filled, with dates in office:
Other civic or community activities we should know about:

A description of your spiritual life, please, including beliefs
 and actions:
Your participation in organized religion: church(es), loca-
 tion(s), pastors:

The most enjoyable trip taken in the past two decades, and
 why:
You and your spouse alone:
You alone:

What you do in your spare or free time:
If you had all the money, energy, skill, and time needed,
 three things you would do right now:
Given the same conditions, three things you'd like to do
 when you are 65:

Things you do for exercise, with hours per week for each:
Accomplishments in the exercise or sports fields:
Writing you have done that has been published, with de-
 tails:
Writing you have done for your own or family enjoyment:
Personal difficulties overcome (details please):

At 45, your thoughts about life in general in the U.S. at the present time:

And your thoughts about the world:

The positive changes you'd like to see happen both immediately and in the future:

From the age perspective of 45, your biggest personal regret so far:

Major step or two you would do differently:

Best decision(s) made so far:

Advice to share with the reader:

List any health changes or updates (this knowledge could be important to your children or future relatives).

What specific health challenges are you facing:

What medications or treatments are you taking?

What is the prognosis, and how has the ailment or condition progressed?

Who is your current doctor for those treatments?

An open question—"What is the most significant contribution you have made to the world during this time period (or so far), and what's the next contribution you intend to make?"

A quick summary of your past two decades, please:

Remember that life list you started at 15 (or later) of things you absolutely want(ed) to do, see, experience, share, or start during your lifetime? Why not modify it, check things off, or add new items to it now?

Anything else you'd like to share at 45?

At age 65 (or ___), or when Social Security normally begins:

(Add any additional comments you wish after each category. Can you provide digital photos of the key events or people of this time period to augment or help illustrate your accounts.)

An update please on your marital history: spouse(s), children by each, stepchildren, age of each now:

Also, please, the same information for grandchildren and great-grandchildren:

Where you have resided the past 20 years, with addresses:

Besides your spouse, others of your family who lived there with you:

Sadly, burial dates and sites of direct family members:

Assuming you may live 25+ more years, share your major life contributions so far (other than your children or spouse):

Honors you have received since 45:

Vocational changes since 45:

Position/firm where you feel you made the greatest impact—please describe:

Update the following areas (or others) you responded to at 45:

Organizations or associations you have taken part in since 45, with offices held:

If not well known, what those groups do:

Civic elected offices you have filled, with dates in office:

Other civic or community activities we should know about:

A description of your spiritual life, please, including beliefs and actions:

Your participation in organized religion: church(es), location(s), pastors:

Places you and your family have traveled together:
You and your spouse alone:
You alone:
The most enjoyable trip taken in the past two decades, and why:

What you do in your spare or free time:
If you had all the money, energy, skill, and time needed, three things you would do right now:
Things you do for exercise, with hours per week for each:
Accomplishments in the exercise or sports fields:
Writing you have done that has been published, with details:
Writing you have done for your own or family enjoyment:
Personal difficulties overcome (details please):

New pets in the past two decades:

At 65, your thoughts about life in general in the U.S. at the present time:
And your thoughts about the world:
The positive changes you'd like to see happen both immediately and in the future:

From the age perspective of 65, your biggest personal regrets so far:
Major step or two you would do differently:
Best decision(s) made so far:
Advice to share with the reader:

List any health changes or updates (this knowledge could be important to your children or future relatives).
What specific health challenges are you facing:

What medications or treatments are you taking?
What is the prognosis, and how has the ailment or condi-
tion progressed?
Who is your current doctor for those treatments?

An open question—"What is the most significant contribution you have made to the world during this time period (or
so far), and what's the next contribution you intend to
make?"

A quick summary of your past two decades, please:

Remember that life list you started at 15 (or later) of things
you absolutely want(ed) to do, see, experience, share, or
start during your lifetime? Why not modify it, check things
off, or add new items to it now?

Do you have a special Dream List to give purpose and joy
to your post-65 (or ___) years:

Anything else you would like to share at 65 (or ___)?

Any time after 65 (or ___):

Simply add any commentary or update you wish at any
time, but please do not modify earlier text. Please add your
age at the time that the change or update is made.

If additions (no changes in the original postings) are made
by others with your expressed permission or after your
passing, would those please be done in *italics*, with the
name of the person making the addition(s), the date, and
their relationship to you.

How should this information be submitted?

The idea is to keep personal information (and all other) data current but also to minimize the time, effort, and skill required to get updates posted by using a uniform, agreed-upon format.

A submission guideline would provide a template with the information sought for each section, plus instructions on how it should be prepared and digitally sent.

In the case of the "Personal Information Repository," for example, the Director or the Family Board might review the lists for the various age plateaus above to decide which items to retain, which to modify, and which to delete.

All material should be sent in readily usable fashion.

Finally, it might ask that the new copy be sent as an attachment to an email, making certain that the file has the submitter's name (Billy Smiles) and the category where the file will appear (Personal Information) at the top so the posting can be done as smoothly and quickly as possible.

What about editing?

"You mean that somebody will actually change what I submit?"

Yep, but only if it needs it.

Most of the edited changes will be corrected typos!

Editing is a quandary because nobody likes to get edited yet nobody wants a stupid misspelling sitting on the website forever just because they weren't aware that "Appril" lost the second "p" sometime before the first Smile crossed the Atlantic, Pacific, or Rio Grande.

Here are some ideas that might be considered:

- Anything handwritten and scanned stays as it is. That is likely to be part of the Ancestral Family Tree and part of its charm is the way things were spelled in the "jolley olde 1700s."

- But in all digital info submitted by the family members, if the Director finds misspelled words or contradictory data (differing birthdates or names, for example), the Director will ask the submitter if the spellings should be corrected or the contradictions resolved before it is posted, and then will follow the submitter's dictate. Thus whatever is posted is done with the submitter's acceptance, right or wrong.

- Another decision for the Family Board or Director: if another family member wants to correct a date or offer a differing factual observation, can that be entered into the person's website data base, in parentheses and italics, followed by that other person's name at the date of entry? For example, if Luigi Smiles says that Belinda Smiles (his ex-wife but a family member nonetheless) was born in Joplin in 1908, can she (through the Director) send a correction that is listed after Luigi's first comment, like *(You've got in wrong, Luigi: it was Oklahoma City in 1911. Belinda Smiles Johnson, 2005)*? Or would that be limited to *(Oklahoma City, 1911. Belinda Smiles Johnson, 2005)*? Or not permitted at all?

- The biggest hassle comes when the material submitted is vague, rambling, or nearly unintelligible. Two schools of thought: (1) even family members have a right to be vague, rambling, or unintelligible, and it is their page and their contribution, so it stands as it is, or (2) the Director might suggest to the person an alternative way of saying the same thing that wouldn't be at least all three, and hopefully will be lucid, enlightening, and maybe even brilliant. The submitter would have a choice of how it would be listed. Often the person will suggest some compromise. Ultimately, whatever the submitter agrees to is how it appears.

- Except when it is blatantly offensive or utterly insane. Then it is the decision of the Family Board or the Director. Blatantly offensive doesn't refer to the person's observations or religious or political beliefs (or lack of), for example. It refers to totally unacceptable language, negative references to others in the family, or anything that would frighten away other family members or jeopardize the continuity of the your living family tree. Utter insanity should require no further definition; if it does, that makes no sense at all.

Sample Personal Information

(Birth Sheet)

EDNA LOUISE BALLOU

Prepared and submitted by Ann Ballou (2/15/2007)

Complete name of baby:	Edna Louise Ballou
Origin(s) of baby's name(s):	Edna in honor of Ann's paternal grandmother (Edna Elsen, 77 at the time of the baby's birth and living in Gary, Indiana). The name Louise sounded good with Edna.
Date of birth:	2/6/2007
Time of birth:	6:27 p.m. CST
Length (height) at birth:	20 inches
Weight at birth:	6 lbs. 6 ozs
Where born?	Roselee Hospital, Lincoln, Wisconsin (Cheese County)
Delivering doctor's name:	Dr. Loretta Washington

Family in attendance at birth:	Ann, Ed Jr., and Lora Ballou; Lydia Smiles
Godparents:	None
Where the parents lived at time of birth:	67 W Wicket St, Apt. 12, Lincoln, WI
Name/age of mother:	Ann (Elden) Ballou (23)
Name/age of father:	Edward Ballou Jr. (24)
Living grandparents:	(Paternal) Lora (56) and Edward (56) Ballou, at 166 Elm Park Drive, Lincoln, WI; (Maternal) Barry (59) and Elizabeth (57) Elden, at RR 16, Box 454, Elkhorn, WI
Living great-grandparents:	(Paternal) William (78) and Wanda (74) Smiles at 3789 Fourth St., Park Plaines, IL; (Maternal) Edna (77) Elden, 554 Rushes Road, Gary, IN
Describe where and when labor first began:	"I was folding laundry about 4:30 p.m. and Ed had just come home."
How did the mother get to the hospital?	Ed drove Ann in a 1991 Ford truck
Any health issues?	None. Healthy as a horse!
Was the baby born with hair?	A wisp of brown hair
Teeth?	The baby was utterly toothless
Other unique characteristics?	None
What family members live at home at the birth?	Mother (Ann) and father (Ed Jr.)

Other observations about the
baby's birth or earliest days

"I had heard that the first baby takes 10-15 hours of labor so we just poked along and didn't call Dr. Washington for an hour. What a shock it was to suddenly have heavy contractions every minute. So we called her right back and Ed lifted me up into the truck and he drove like an old lady all the way to the hospital. I think he thought he'd shake the baby right out! The rest was so fast I hardly had time to suffer…"

Ann Ballou, Edna's mother

"Ann's got that right. Cautious driving isn't my trademark and half of me said to drive like Petty, but I sure in hell didn't want the baby to be born on the town square with me as the mid-wife! She was a real trouper and between labor pains could hardly stop laughing."

Ed Ballou Jr., Edna's father

"Isn't she one pretty baby? She looks like she was born de-wrinkled! Our first grandchild!"

Elizabeth (Bet) Elden, Ann's mother

"How does she have such little fingers? She squeaks like a baby monkey."

Reginald Smiles, III, Edna's cousin (at 4)

Sample Personal Information

(Age 15 Sheet)

PAUL LEE SMILES

Prepared and submitted by Paul Smiles (8/24/2007)
Paul was 14 and just entering high school.

Where are you living now?	98 N. Third Ave., Park Plaines, IL 60016
Who else is living in that home?	Reginald and Belinda Smiles (parents), Belinda and Rita Smiles (sisters)
Until now what schools have you attended?	Central School for kindergarten to grade 6; at Lee and Lilac Sts., now site of Costco warehouses; Jefferson Jr. High School for grades 7-8, at 16 West Elgin Avenue, all in Park Plaines, IL
Your grade school teachers before high school?	(K) Miss Laster, (1) Miss Johnson, (2) Ms. Oakes, (3) Ms. Goatas, (4) Ms. Kilpatrick, (5) Miss Doherty, (6) Ms. Weeks; 7-8, homeroom, Mr. Lesh

Favorite teacher?	Miss Doherty. She was very strict but lots of fun and liked to join in the games and take the class to picnics by the river
What sports have you played since entering school?	A lot of sandlot baseball, basketball, and touch football. I was a catcher in the Little League and on the junior high school team. Played basketball in eighth grade on junior high school team
Your favorite sports teams?	Chicago Cubs, White Sox, Bears, and Bulls
Do/can you cycle five miles?	Yes, we would ride to forest preserves that far away, have lunch, then come back lots of times
Do/can you swim?	Yes: crawl, backstroke, and breast stroke. I can also dive off the board, front or back dives
Do/can you cook a full meal?	Sure. I can eat it too!
Can you speak a foreign language?	Some Spanish because I get to talk a lot with my Mom's relatives and some of them don't speak English
Can you hold a tune?	I sang in the chorus at JHS
Can you dance?	Jitterbug and fox trot
Do you play a musical instrument?	Violin, took lessons for four years, played in the JHS orchestra
What is your favorite musical star or group?	I like country music
What other activities do you enjoy?	I collect autographs of baseball stars and I keep score for the men's rec night league softball games.

Who are your five favorite friends (about your age) right now?	Lenny Grazen, Dray Lu, Billy Smith, Marilee Heine, and Sheila Tassle
Which states or countries you have visited?	I've been in every state that touches Illinois, plus Kentucky and Iowa
Are you baptized?	No
What do you want to do when you are fully grown up?	Maybe write sports or play with the Cubs or Sox
What job or position would you most want to have when you're an adult?	It would be great to work with a newspaper or a magazine like *Sports Illustrated*. Or work outside, like a forest ranger
Which adults outside your family do you most admire?	Two of my former coaches (Mr. Litlivia and Mr. Ollie Brown) and a lot of the TV comedians
What's the dumbest thing a person your age could do?	Get married at 14! Or take some addictive drugs
If a long-lost uncle wanted to know what you are like, how would you describe yourself right now?	I'm short, read a lot, ride my bike around to shoot baskets or play ball, I am pretty funny, and I'm very honest—you believe that?
What is the prettiest place you have ever visited?	Maybe the Wisconsin Dells in the spring just at dark
Your three favorite TV shows?	Smallville; the Cubs/White Sox, Bears, and Bulls telecasts
Your three favorite CDs or DVDs?	No favorites but I collect and listen to comedians do their one-person shows, on CD or video. I like Paul Rodriguez a lot.

Describe your mother	My mother is Rosa Smiles, and she has 100 cousins all from Mexico or here in the States for 30-50 years. They are a lot of fun, always joking and kidding. They are teaching me to speak Spanish too. Mom is real involved with Belinda, Rita, and me, and if we play in a game or do anything she will come and watch, and usually drag along some cousins. She cooks real well, both Mexican and American food. She also sews real well, and makes dresses for the girls. She and my Dad kid each other a lot. They met at a church singles picnic when he was 35 and she was 26.
Describe your father	He was married once before (to Agnes) and they had a son Barry who I always knew as my big brother since he lived with us. My Dad works real hard and is also very handy, repairing things and keeping the cars running. He's not very good at sports but he likes to see us play. Mostly he's real hard on us when it comes to studies. If you get a B you have to spend extra time on that subject, and when you get a C he starts tutoring, which none of us wants. He likes to garden, fish, read, and play computer games.

Describe your living grand-parents	My grandparents are Grandpa Bill (78) and Grandma Wanda (74). They live a few miles away. I used to cut their lawn and keep up their house. We see them a lot on holidays, and we used to spend a week at their house every summer. They are very proper people who live in a small house and neither drives much anymore, except to the store or church. I think they are poor. Their TV is still black and white, and they usually listen to the radio, and play cards or dominos. They both used to smoke but now they hate it and won't let tobacco or spirits into their house. My mother's parents died when I was about five, and I only remember my grandmother Maria a little bit. But my mother has told us a lot about both of them, and their brothers and sisters are still alive and we see them, as well as the Smiles uncles and aunts. I have a lot of living relatives!
Anything else you would like to share at 14?	That's it! I'll be back at 25.

Family Directory

This section on the website couldn't be more obvious: it's a contact map to where the rest of the family is hiding, physically and digitally, and how you can find or reach them.

While most of the website is historical, this is for everyday use, and includes only those living members who want to be in contact and/or contacted by other kin. Moreover, while the other LFT sections request an occasional updating or a faithful posting at certain age plateaus, a directory is only effective if it is kept current.

A Map

Indeed, a Family Directory may begin with an actual map of the U.S., at least, with a numbered code telling where each of the family members resides. Reginald and Rosa Smiles, for example, number 4 in order of the family list alphabetically, live in Park Plaines, so on the national mainland map a 4 is located about 40 miles NW of Chicago, with the other numbers scattered by their residences. Why do this? Some react or respond well to such a visual rendering. And it's easier to grasp the family spread and a lot more fun for the kids to find family friends on a map. It also might be fun to see a copy of this map taken, say, every Christmas, for the past 100 years to see the historical spread of the Smiles clan.

Those are also especially useful when visiting kin.

The Directory List

Here is where the vital contact information about each member is found. That would include the person's full name, relationship to the core couple, full residence address, home telephone, cell telephone, perhaps work phone, fax number, email address, and website connection. These require frequent updating to keep current, particularly the cell phones.

There are several choices that the Director or Family Board have to make at the outset. The two most important are whether they want access to the addresses limited and how they want the Family Directory list organized.

We'll discuss public accessibility again in a moment.

Regarding organization, the most obvious format is used in an example that follows this chapter in the Smiles Family Directory. That is to list the name and relationship of each family member in alphabetical order, followed by a fill-in table with the desired data provided by the person listed or by another family member (mostly for very young children or the newly born). Blank items in the table mean that the person can't be reached that way (they may not have a fax, for example) or that they prefer not to be.

Other formats usually include similar information presented differently.

In one case, the names and accompanying data might be lumped together by family clusters. In our example, there would be seven such discrete listings: five family members living at Third Avenue in Park Plaines, four each in Olha and at Elm Street in Lincoln, three each at Fourth St. in Park Plaines, one at Amber Ct. in Park Plaines, one on Wicket Street in Lincoln, and one in Nebraska. In this case, the head of each family unit (distinguished by the home they share) would be listed, followed by the others living there, with each person's unique addresses (usually their cell phones and email addresses) also listed with their name and relationship to the core couple.

Here is one example of how such a cluster might appear:

◆ **Barry Smiles**, (4), son of Reginald and Agnes Smiles, 57 Old Orchard Lane, Olha, IL 60099, (811) 578-8684, cell (811) 578-9057, work (811) 578-2098, fax (811) 578-5034, BarryS@airwave.com.

> * **Dolores Smiles** (Gunderson), wife of Barry, cell (811) 578-7770, BarryS@airwave.com.
>
> * **Iris Smiles**, daughter of Barry and Dolores.
>
> * **Reginald II**, son of Barry and Dolores.

The number after Barry Smiles' name indicates where the house is located on the map. It assumes that all four family members listed live at the same address.

As each person gets a new or different means of contact that they wish to enter, or they wish to change what is already posted, they simply inform the Director. For example, if Mary Jean gets her own cell phone, that would be added. If Billy goes on to college, he will have several new additions plus a new address, like a cell phone and the dorm or fraternity fax.

When does a person escape the family linking? When they move out and live elsewhere!

The groups would likely be listed alphabetically by the group leader.

Other listing formats might be by age, by living family tree, or by state, then city.

The trick is to find a format that all can understand, then stick with it!

Who gets to see this valuable information?

The family members, of course, though you can even limit that by posting only what you want them to know.

But you may not want this list in front of every opportunistic entrepreneur visiting the web, so this may well be the most important page requiring password entrance. That's a family decision, of course, but as long as everybody in the family knows the password (and keeps it private), that should provide enough protection so that the list can be used when needed, particularly during holiday season.

How do you first post your Family Directory information?

The Director will tell you how it should be sent. You will almost certainly be asked to provide at least this information in this order: your full name, relationship to the core couple, full residence address, home telephone, cell telephone, perhaps work phone, fax number, email address, and website connection. If you are providing it for other family members too, just put each member's information on separate lines.

How do you update your information?

Since the changes must be hand-entered once the list exists and is visible at the website, just send the changes to the Director by email, being sure to include your full name and telling what old fact you are changing with what new fact, or what new information should be added. Be patient. A few days later, or sooner, you'll be listed whole again!

Sample Family Directory

SMILES FAMILY DIRECTORY

Ann (Elden) Ballou

Relationship	Wife of Edward Ballou Jr.
Residence Address	67 W Wicket St., Apt 12, Lincoln, WI 53455
Home Telephone	(267) 323-1177
Cell Telephone	
Work Phone	
Fax	(267) 323-5568
Email Address	AnnB@badger.net
Website Address	www.EddiesBarandGrill.com

Edna Louise Ballou

Relationship	Daughter of Ed Jr. and Ann Ballou
Residence Address	67 W Wicket St., Apt 12, Lincoln, WI 53455
Home Telephone	(267) 323-1177
Fax	(267) 323-5568
Website Address	

Edward Ballou

Relationship	Husband of Lora (Smiles) Ballou
Residence Address	166 Elm Park Dr., Lincoln, WI 53455
Home Telephone	(267) 323-4567
Cell Telephone	(267) 323-1234
Work Phone	(267) 323-4422
Fax	(267) 323-5566
Email Address	EdBOne@badger.com
Website Address	

Edward Ballou Jr.

Relationship	Son of Edward and Lora Ballou
Residence Address	67 W Wicket St., Apt 12, Lincoln, WI 53455
Home Telephone	(267) 323-1177
Cell Telephone	(267) 323-0805
Work Phone	(267) 323-5567
Fax	(267) 323-5566
Email Address	EdBJr@badger.net
Website Address	www.EddiesBarandGrill.com

Lora (Smiles) Ballou

Relationship	Daughter of Bill and Wanda Smiles
Residence Address	166 Elm Park Dr., Lincoln, WI 53455
Home Telephone	(267) 323-4567
Cell Telephone	
Work Phone	(267) 323-6783
Fax	(267) 323-5566
Email Address	LoraB@badger.com
Website Address	

Lorlta Ballou

Relationship	Daughter of Edward and Lora Ballou
Residence Address	166 Elm Park Dr., Lincoln, WI 53455
College Address	564 Ghent Towers, Madison, WI 53711
Home Telephone	(267) 323-4567
Cell Telephone	(267) 323-9845
College Phone	(564) 407-8572
Home Fax	(267) 323-5566
Email Address	LLBallou@badger.com
College Fax	(564) 008-9080
Website Address	

Tom Ballou

Relationship	Son of Edward and Lora Ballou
Residence Address	166 Elm Park Dr., Lincoln, WI 53455
Home Telephone	(267) 323-4567
Cell Telephone	(267) 323-5131
Work Phone	(267) 323-1659
Fax	(267) 323-5566
Email Address	TommyB@badger.com
Website Address	www.Tommy'sTrucks.com

Agnes (Lagsworth) Smiles

Relationship	Ex-Wife of Reginald Smiles
Residence Address	8080 Main St., Brushfire, NE 68114
Home Telephone	(691) 577-1218
Cell Telephone	
Work Phone	(691) 577-9524
Fax	
Email Address	
Website Address	

Barry Smiles

Relationship	Son of Reginald and Agnes Smiles
Residence Address	57 Old Orchard Lane, Olha, IL 60099
Home Telephone	(811) 578-8684
Cell Telephone	(811) 578-9057
Work Phone	(811) 578-2098
Fax	(811) 578-5034
Email Address	BarryS@airwave.com
Website Address	

Belinda Smiles

Relationship	Daughter of Reginald and Rosa Smiles
Residence Address	98 N. Third Ave., Park Plaines, IL 60016
Home Telephone	(847) 123-6845
Cell Telephone	(847) 123-6632
Work Phone	
Fax	(847) 123- 4736
Email Address	BelindaS@esquire.net
Website Address	

Dolores (Gunderson) Smiles

Relationship	Wife of Barry Smiles
Residence Address	57 Old Orchard Lane, Olha, IL 60099
Home Telephone	(811) 578-8684
Cell Telephone	(811) 578-7770
Work Phone	
Fax	(811) 578-5034
Email Address	BarryS@airwave.com
Website Address	

Iris Smiles

Relationship	Daughter of Barry and Dolores Smiles
Residence Address	57 Old Orchard Lane, Olha, IL 60099
Home Telephone	(811) 578-8684
Cell Telephone	
Work Phone	
Fax	(811) 578-5034
Email Address	
Website Address	

Lydia Smiles

Relationship	Daughter of Bill and Wanda Smiles
Residence Address	3789 Fourth St., Park Plaines, IL 60016
Home Telephone	(847) 123-4567
Cell Telephone	(847) 123-6677
Work Phone	(847) 123-8899
Fax	(847) 123-1234
Email Address	AuntLydia@esquire.net
Website Address	

Candi Smiles

Relationship	Daughter of Reginald and Agnes Smiles
Residence Address	564 Amber Ct., Apt. 2B., Park Plaines, IL 60016
Home Telephone	(847) 123-9576
Cell Telephone	
Work Phone	(847) 123-9008
Fax	
Email Address	Candi@bighouse.net
Website Address	

Paul Smiles

Relationship	Son of Reginald and Rosa Smiles
Residence Address	98 N. Third Ave., Park Plaines, IL 60016
Home Telephone	(847) 123-6845
Cell Telephone	(847) 123-9686
Work Phone	
Fax	(847) 123- 4736
Email Address	PaulS@esquire.net
Website Address	

Reginald Smiles

Relationship	Son of Bill and Wanda Smiles
Residence Address	98 N. Third Ave., Park Plaines, IL 60016
Home Telephone	(847) 123-6845
Cell Telephone	(847) 123-8600
Work Phone	(847) 123-5569
Fax	(847) 123- 4736
Email Address	Reginald@esquire.nct
Website Address	

Reginald Smiles II

Relationship	Son of Barry and Dolores Smiles
Residence Address	57 Old Orchard Lane, Olha, IL 60099
Home Telephone	(811) 578-8684
Cell Telephone	
Work Phone	
Fax	(811) 578-5034
Email Address	
Website Address	

Rosa (Suarez) Smiles

Relationship	Wife of Reginald Smiles
Residence Address	98 N. Third Ave., Park Plaines, IL 60016
Home Telephone	(847) 123-6845
Cell Telephone	(847) 123-9786
Work Phone	(847) 123-3377
Fax	(847) 123- 4736
Email Address	RosaS@esquire.net
Website Address	

Rita Smiles

Relationship	Daughter of Reginald and Rosa Smiles
Residence Address	98 N. Third Ave., Park Plaines, IL 60016
Home Telephone	(847) 123-6845
Cell Telephone	(847) 123-7922
Work Phone	
Fax	(847) 123- 4736
Email Address	RitaS@esquire.net
Website Address	

William "Bill" Smiles

Relationship	Core father
Residence Address	3789 Fourth St., Park Plaines, IL 60016
Home Telephone	(847) 123-4567
Cell Telephone	
Work Phone	
Fax	(847) 123-1234
Email Address	BigBill@esquire.net
Website Address	

Wanda (Lynch) Smiles

Relationship	Core mother
Residence Address	3789 Fourth St., Park Plaines, IL 60016
Home Telephone	(847) 123-4567
Cell Telephone	
Work Phone	
Fax	(847) 123-1234
Email Address	MamaWanda@esquire.net
Website Address	

Want to update, change, or remove anything on your page?

Just contact the Director (Lora Ballou) at LoraB@badger.com.

Key Date List

Ever wonder when your brother's birthday is? Or your parent's anniversary?

The Key Date List takes care of that. It puts in one place on the family website all of the key dates you might ever need to know about your kin—or even your own spouse!

What's included? Anything you want to share, but certainly birth dates of every family member and the anniversary dates of those still married (plus those widowed, if they wish, until they remarry). Those are permanent fixtures of each member of the living family.

What else? Perhaps…

- Baptism, bar mitzvah, or other religious equivalent
- Graduation from junior high school or middle school, high school, college, grad school, or equivalent vocational, military, police, or legal institutes
- Marriage
- Major operations
- Family reunion picnic

Some of the listings, as mentioned, will be permanent; others, like those above, will be added as soon as the person sharing the information has a confirmed date. The list may be posted for the year in question—or two, the current year and the coming year.

How complete will the listings be? Another decision. At least the date and the occasion, perhaps with more information that would help the others understand or attend. The name of the person honored or acknowledged must be there too for many in the family will use this Key Date List to call or send a card, email, or gift.

The "Key Date Listings" differ from the "Tip of the Hat List" in a significant way, although some of the occasions listed will be the same. Here, the event is simply listed, with perhaps some supplementary information. On the "Tip of the Hat" List the person is honored, usually in some detail, for having actually realized the achievement.

What might a Key Date List look like?

Whatever you want it to look like, really. It's your family list, and its form is the family invention. It might be a conventional fact list, black and white, properly indented. But it might be in colors, with each activity a different hue. It might make noise. It may display artwork, have moving features, or have fancy borders. That's up to you.

Here's a simple, unadorned idea of how the March listings might appear, to show how contents might be handled. A full-year example follows this chapter.

MARCH

3	Anniversary	Bill Sr. and Wanda Smiles	Can you believe 53?
5	Birthday	Bill Smiles, Sr.	Still as strong as a horse...
6	Birthday	Wanda Smiles	And as wild as a filly!
14	Birthday	Lydia Smiles	

The "Key Date List" is kept intact throughout the year, and might be archived (kept in a file that can be reread at any time in the future). Imagine 200 years from now being able to go back and see the contemporary date when your beloved great-great-great-grandmother was married, then later read the full details on the archived "Tip of the Hat" list of that same year!

The list for the next year will pick up the permanent items, until the person having birthdays, alas, passes or the anniversaries are removed by dissolution, divorce, or a request of one of the parties involved.

How do you get listed—or unlisted?

By simply giving the needed information to the Director by email, since it must be hand entered. Just be sure you have all the facts needed so the listing doesn't have to be added to or amended repeatedly, and that you fully identify yourself. The exceptions are tentative listings, like marriages, where the facts are often planned much earlier than the final details are known.

Sample Key Date List

2007

Don't forget to tell the Director about
engagements, marriages, births, baptisms,
and all school or academy graduations!

(Contact the Director at LoraB@badger.com)

JANUARY

3	Birthday	Lorita Ballou	Lorrie can finally drink legally!

FEBRUARY

6	Birthday	Edna Ballou	Just born in 2007!
9	Birthday	Rosa Smiles	

MARCH

3	Anniversary	Bill Sr. and Wanda Smiles	Can you believe 53?
5	Birthday	Bill Smiles Sr.	Still strong as a horse…
6	Birthday	Wanda Smiles	And wild as a filly!
14	Birthday	Lydia Smiles	

APRIL

16	Birthday	Dolores Smiles	
26	Birthday	Maria Smiles	

MAY

6	Anniversary	Ed and Lora Ballou	Their 35th!
22	Birthday	Paul Smiles	Scary thought: Paul will drive soon!

JUNE

10	Jr. H.S. Graduation	Paul Smiles	Check later for exact date and location
14	Birthday	William Smiles Jr.	Bill will be 26 this year!
17-8	Family Reunion Picnic	All are invited!	Lions Park Campground and Conference Room, Park Plaines, Illinois

JULY

1	Birthday	Lora Ballou	
7	Anniversary	Barry and Dolores Smiles	

AUGUST

16	Birthday	Reginald Smiles II	Older still than Iris!
25	Birthday	Belinda Smiles	A dozen candles!

SEPTEMBER

14	Birthday	Ann Ballou	
29	Birthday	Barry Smiles	

OCTOBER

11	Birthday	Rita Smiles	Two aces!
14	Birthday	Edward Ballou	

NOVEMBER

11	Anniversary	Reggie and Rosa Smiles	
25	Birthday	Tom Ballou	
26	Birthday	Edward Ballou Jr.	

DECEMBER

6	Birthday	Reginald Smiles	
8	Birthday	Agnes Smiles	
10	Anniversary	Ed Jr. and Ann Ballou	Two years and still hitched!
17	Birthday	Iris Smiles	Baby Iris is two!

Family Registry

The contents and purpose of this section are almost self-explanatory, although there may be some redundancy with other sections of your family living tree website, like the "Tip of the Hat" Acclamation (where the good news is announced), the "In Memoriam" Announcement (where the bad news is shared), and the Annual Family Summary (where all the news is repeated and bound together by year).

In short, this is where the details regarding a family member's birth, baptism, marriage, and death are "officially" listed for family (or public) perusal. (The four events mentioned are the most common social stages that most experience in life, although "baptism" might be omitted or changed to correspond to the family's different religious beliefs.)

But it's your living family tree and you, the Director, or the Family Board may wish to "register" more events—or fewer. Or more or less information might be sought than the sample below suggests.

Why bother to repeat the same information?

Each category serves a different purpose, and if one simply wants the details about Sylvester Smiles a decade or century hence, it will be much faster and easier to call up the Family Registry and find all four events listed in one place (with the names probably in alphabetical order and the events chronological) than to have to rummage through all of the acclamations, announcements, and summaries for 60, 80, or 680 years to find Sylvester.

How is the Registry Information gathered?

Since this is a permanent listing of major family events to be kept as long as your living family tree is maintained and shared (and longer, inactively, in archives should others wish to use it later), the only requisite is that all registrations include the same basic information.

Once the needed information is established for each category, if the person informing the Director about the person and event for either the "Tip of the Hat" Acclamation or the "In Memoriam" Announcement includes all of the needed data, that's it. The Director will complete both functions with the same data. And if anything is missing, unclear, or erroneous, the Director will resolve that issue before posting either entry.

Who informs the Director?

Need it be a specific person? Most likely it will be a parent for a birth or baptism, though the parent(s) might ask a grandparent or anybody else to get the information to the Director quickly. One imagines that the betrothed family member would share those good tidings, though again it may be a greatly relieved parent! About the deceased? Usually a child or mate. Yet as long as the information is accurate and timely, it hardly matters who is the conveyor of the news.

Cross-references might be useful too

In the example that follows we are using the birth of Edna Louise Ballou as the event to be recorded in the Family Registry. The Smiles family will first hear of this joyful arrival through a "Tip of the Hat" Acclamation, which will also contain one or many photos, the same basic information somewhat rephrased, and commentaries from the parents and others.

Doesn't it then make huge sense to indicate in the Family Registry that more information about the same event can be found in the Smiles Living Family Tree?

Sample Family Registry

BALLOU, EDNA LOUISE

Birth

Parents: Ann and Ed Ballou, Jr
Time and date of birth: 6:27 p.m. on February 6, 2007
City and state or nation: Lincoln, Wisconsin
Location of birth: Roselee Hospital
Primary physician: Dr. Loretta Washington
Weight: 6 lbs 6 ozs
Height or length: 20"
Additional information: Tip of the Hat (2/7/07), Annual Family
    Summary (2007)

"Tip of the Hat" Acclamation

No small part of your living family tree is recording now and preserving forever the achievements and recognitions of one's life, then sharing them with others in the family both now and later.

That's where the "Tip of the Hat" fits in, though you may, of course, call it anything else you wish. Its purpose is to record those special things you do in a special way.

What's worthy of a "tip of the hat"?

Again, a decision for a Family Board or the Director.

But you might begin with some milestone recognitions that uniformly apply to all in the family, like births, baptisms, diplomas received (perhaps from high school, college, trade or vocational school, master's degree, doctorate), and marriage.

A second category might be called "Exceptional Achievements," into which all sorts of extraordinary, important acknowledgments might fit, like appointment to high or key positions, a Nobel Prize, the school honor roll or dean's list, election as mayor or to the House of Representatives, signing a major league contract, almost anything significantly above the ordinary.

How might the "tip of the hat" pages look?

They might vary by the acknowledgment. A birth page might look far different than, say, a school Honor Roll list or a marriage page. Three examples might show the wide variety possible.

A **birth page**, for example, might contain the full name of the child; the derivation of each name; the parents' names; the minute, hour, and date of the birth; the location where the birth took place; the name of the doctor(s) delivering, and other facts worth sharing.

It would also surely include a full picture of the new baby, plus perhaps several more photos of the parents, family, friends, and events at the time of the birth.

There might be a box each for commentary by the mother and the father, or others.

There might be another box for a 50- or 100-word summary.

The page might be enclosed in a special design template (or frame) signifying birth.

An **Honor Roll** list might be far less visual and smaller, but no less important (particularly to the younger students it is designed to inspire). It might be a simple list, something like what follows:

The "code" below refers to how the "honor roll" information is received or verified, like "HR" for honor roll and "DL" for dean's list. There might be a key at the bottom of the roll to help decipher that column. There also might be a way to distinguish the "honor roll," which often means a B average or better from "high honors," which may signify all (or nearly all) A's.

SMILES FAMILY 2007 HONOR ROLL

Student's Name	Code	Year in School	Semes- ter or Year	Times on Honor Roll
Rita Smiles (Davies Grade School)	HR	6	Fall / 2007	5
Rita Smiles (Davies Grade School)	HR	6	Spring/ 2007	6
Rosa Smiles (Rand C.C.)	DL	Soph.	Spring/ 2007	3
Tom Ballou (Northern Illinois U.)	DL	Sr.	Spring /2007	14

A **marriage page** would also be different. See that in the Sample "Tip of the Hat" at the end of this section.

Where are "Tip of the Hat" pages stored?

Probably in a special section for one year, although two years might work better for Honor Rolls (since the year honored might actually cover two, through the winter session).

Then the pages could be accessibly archived and featured (in summary) in the respective personal information sections. Or there could be permanent "tip of the hat" archives, for marriage, birth, graduation, and so on, with the newest first, descending from the current date.

Could the pages be removed at the person's request? For example, a marriage so festively honored and recorded sadly gone sour? Another decision, but a historical compromise is surely possible. Unless the person requesting the item to be withdrawn asks for it to be subsequently reinstated, it might be kept on a private (Director access only) page and returned to view at the person's death, so it is available for future generations. (Or it might be removed altogether as long as the facts remain on the personal information page.)

How are the "Tip of the Hat" pages submitted?

As many ways as there are pages, one guesses.

There could be template or content pages for the standard categories (sample content pages follow), with Honor Roll information simply emailed to the Director (unless that soul is so hard-hearted as to demand a faxed copy of the school confirmation letter!) What would you email? The same information that's on the page itself, like the person to be listed, school, code, the year in school when the person was on the honor roll in question, the time that covers (semester, quarter, year), and your name. I presume the Director will fill in the number of times that student has now been on the family Honor Roll.

What might the most probable pages list, in addition to photos (and perhaps audio, music, or video—see the chapters that follow about non-text submission)?

A **birth page** we already mentioned:

- the full name of the child
- the derivation of each name
- the parents' names
- the minute, hour, and date of the birth
- the location where the birth took place
- the name(s) of the delivering doctor(s)
- other facts worth sharing (like family members in attendance)
- commentary by the mother and the father, or others
- a 50- or 100-word summary

A **baptism** page?

- the full name of the baptized child
- the parents' names
- the location of the baptism
- the church into which the child was baptized, with full address and religious denomination
- the clergy performing the baptism
- the hour and date of the baptism
- other facts worth sharing (like family members in attendance)
- commentary by the mother and the father, or others
- a 50- or 100-word summary

A **diploma** or **achievement** page?

- the full name of the student receiving the diploma or award
- the degree or award being given
- the institution or group giving the diploma or award
- any extraordinary honors or special acknowledgements given the student at the ceremony
- where and when the degree ceremony took place, if attended by the student
- if appropriate, the academic, trade, or vocational field in which the degree is awarded
- other facts worth sharing (like family members in attendance)
- commentary by the student
- a 50- or 100-word summary

A marriage page?

- the full names of those being married
- the non-Smiles newlywed: where born, when, parents' full names and address(es)
- where and when the ceremony and reception took place
- clergy or person performing the marriage
- full names (and residences) of the marriage party: maid of honor, best man, others
- where the honeymoon was spent
- both marriage participants' family members in attendance
- other facts worth sharing
- commentary by both the bride and the groom
- a 50- or 100-word summary

Incidentally, many of the actual documents related to the "Tip of the Hat," like birth certificates, baptism papers, diplomas, marriage certificates, even high honors sheets, might also be scanned and kept in the "Family Treasures in Print."

For the "Exceptional Achievements" pages, the contents might be participant-driven, with the person receiving the recognition (or the other family member proposing its inclusion) contacting the Director by email and explaining the achievement, the details about it, and all available non-text items (like photos or video) that could be provided. In lieu of a standard template or contents sheet, then, the Director would request any additional information necessary to post the new page.

Sample Tip of the Hat!

A NEW SMILES BABY!

Edna Louise Ballou

Born to Ann and Ed Ballou, Jr.
6:27 p.m. on
February 6, 2007
Roselee Hospital, Lincoln, WI

Baby Edna weighed 6 lbs. 6 ozs,, was 20" long, had a wisp of brown hair, no teeth, and, according to her father, looks just like him! Ann and Ed chose the name "Edna" to honor Ann's grandmother (Edna Elsden, now 77 and living in Gary, Indiana). Louise was chosen because it sounded good with Edna, not because Ed's first girlfriend (we all remember the redhead who was a head taller than him in his freshman year in high school) was named Louise! Edna couldn't wait to enter this world. Ann was in labor barely two hours; they just made it to the Maternity Ward in time. Dr. Loretta Washington was also a close call, arriving just in time to deliver Baby Edna. At the hospital during delivery were Ann (thank God!), Ed Jr., Lora, and Lydia. The paternal grandfather arrived ten minutes later with both of Ann's parents and her youngest sister, Arleta.

COMMENTARIES:

"I had heard that the first baby takes 10-15 hours of labor so we just poked along and didn't call Dr. Washington for an hour. What a shock it was to suddenly have heavy contractions every minute. So we called her right back and Ed lifted me up into the truck and he drove like an old lady all the way to the hospital. I think he thought he'd shake the baby right out! The rest was so fast I hardly had time to suffer..."

Ann Ballou, Edna's mother

"Ann's got that right. Cautious driving isn't my trademark and half of me said to drive like Petty, but I sure in the hell didn't want the baby to be born on the town square with me as the midwife! She was a real trouper and between labor pains could hardly stop laughing."

Ed Ballou Jr., Edna's father

"Isn't she one pretty baby? She looks like she was born dewrinkled! Our first grandchild!"

Elizabeth (Bet) Elden, Ann's mother

"How does she have such little fingers? She squeaks like a baby monkey."

Reginald Smiles, III, Edna's cousin (at 4)

"In Memoriam" Announcements

It all comes to this. The unwanted death notice. One hopes the passing is very long in coming but painless and fast when it does, after an abundance of love, joy, purpose, accomplishments, and fun.

Still, death is the price of life, and your living family tree is a proper place to honor the passing with a dignified posting and summary.

Those closest to the person need the summary least—they personally shared the laughter and pride. But kin decades and centuries later seeking genealogical worth and guidance will be the most grateful for whatever three-dimensional insights a living family tree can provide.

The "In Memoriam" page is the starting place, as well as the location where additional substantiation of the person can be found, like the site(s) of more photos, a recording or video, items in print, or some physical creation in the Family Treasure Box.

What is needed for the "In Memoriam" page?

The final design and contents are your decision, but may include this factual information:

- The person's full name (plus any nicknames that person used)
- The time and place of their passing
- The date of their birth and their age when they died

- Details about the funeral ceremony: at least the place it was held, date, and official or clergy attending
- Where the person is buried (to help descendants find it later): plot location, city, state, name under which the person is buried (actual or a nickname), perhaps even a photo of the grave
- A list of direct family members: wife or wives, children (from each), number of grandchildren from children
- a 100- to 200-word summary of the person's key accomplishments, with reference to the more detailed Personal Information page(s) in the family living tree

Which photo is used on the "In Memoriam" page?

If the person doesn't specifically designate a photo that he/she wants used on this page to the Director or a close family member, then it is up to the Director or the closest family member(s) to select the best or most representative of the photos provided or on file.

The choices are usually between the "best," usually mid-life, photo of the person in full health and vigor or a more mature photo taken in later life, although one sometimes sees a photo taken in the coffin. Is there any reason that two photos, if wanted by the closest family member(s), can't be used, one at the person's "best," the other, from later?

For additional photos, references can be made to other pages in the living family tree.

What about short, personal commentaries about the deceased?

Why not let those who knew (and liked) the deceased share positive comments on the "In Memoriam" page in special boxes below the main information? The comments would be placed with those closest by blood to the person first, then in declining proximity.

While (length) space isn't a key factor in a digital file, it might be practical to limit the commentaries to roughly the length of the summary listing of the deceased's accomplishments. It might also be informative for later readers if the person offering the commentary indicated their relationship to the deceased, if any. For example, after a commentary it might say, "Liana Smiles, cousin."

Should others outside the family be allowed to add commentary? A Family Board decision.

How would this information be submitted?

The Director would have a contents format page for "In Memoriam" submissions. It would be similar to the list above about what is needed, plus any additional (or different) information requested. Because the page must be hand composed, the information can be sent either as an attachment to an email or as the text of the email itself. Indicate in that information which photos the deceased (or you) would like used, and if it isn't already posted elsewhere on the living family tree (if so, tell where), you must provide that photo. (See the section about photos.)

Short, personal commentaries should follow the format of other commentaries on a recent "In Memoriam" page and can be submitted as email text. Be certain to include the name of the deceased, your name, and your relationship to the person who has passed.

How quickly must this information be submitted?

So others in the family are quickly aware of the passing, share with the Director (by email or phone) the general details as soon as you can. A partial "In Memoriam" can be posted while the rest is added. The initial information might also be distributed quickly to all family members through a "Family Flash." (See the "Family Flash" chapter.)

A good time to submit the rest of the information is when similar information is sent to the newspaper obituaries. Then if anything is still missing, the Director will request it.

Sample "In Memoriam"

"In Memoriam"

WILLIAM SMILES Jr.

PHOTO	**Bill Smiles** was 24 years old on June 14, 1980 when his 1964 red Chevy convertible blew a tire on what used to be Route 66 near Joliet, Illinois, and collided with a bridge abutment. The funeral service was held at the Ryan Funeral Home in Park Plaines on June 17. Over 1,000 people attended the service and interment, including his parents (Bill and Wanda), his brother Reggie (with his wife Agnes and their infant son Barry), his sister Lydia, and his sister Lora (with her husband Ed). Bill Junior is buried in the nearby Loreen Cemetery in plot 1154, which is located in the northwest corner, row 2.

During grade school, "Billy" played baseball in the Little League (mostly as pitcher and first baseman), rode his bike

everywhere, liked to fish, and collected stamps. He was a Cub
Scout, and later attended Boy Scout camp every winter and
summer.

In high school, Bill was 3.4-average student (4 was A),
played baseball four years, ran track the last two (mostly the
880 and low hurdles), made the Honor Society, and worked
several days a week and most weekends at Dairy Queen and
Howard Johnson restaurants. He bought his first car as a junior.

Bill received a B.A. in business administration at Northern
Illinois University, DeKalb, and had just completed the last
credits of his MBA from the same school a week before the
accident occurred. He was engaged to be married to Betty
Janeson of Princeton, Illinois, at that time. The marriage had
been tentatively set for November, 1980.

Commentaries:

"Billy was my kid brother (six years younger) and from the
moment he learned to ride a bike I just saw him at meals. But
later, when I married Ed, the two of them liked to play catch
and became real good friends, and I got to know him best when
he was in college and used to come to our apartment to use my
typewriter. He had a great sense of humor, wrote well, and sure
loved Betty. What a shock and a loss."

Lora (Smiles) Ballou, Bill's oldest sister

"Billy liked to hear the Cubs games at night, when they
were on the road, but we only had a big family radio and my
folks didn't like baseball, so I secretly let him use my tiny little
electric radio. He'd put it under his pillow. They thought he
was asleep. One night I guess the game went into extra innings
because the pillow got so hot it started on fire! Mom looked

around for that pillow case for about a week. It had a big hole in it and we'd put it in the bottom of the garbage!"

Lydia Smiles, Bill's other sister

"Bill was two years younger than I was but you'd never know it by the way he played ball. He was the best player and I was about the worst but he made sure I always got picked and got to play. He sure liked to read, almost anything, but he didn't want others to see him do it, until he got to college. So you would find him in the goofiest places reading books—in the basement on a pile of clothes to be washed, in a closet, even in the attic. And he was always good for a free hamburger when he worked at Dairy Queen. I suspect he paid for them himself. They were a dime then."

Reggie Smiles, Bill's brother

"Bill was my best friend at NIU. We shared a room in the dorm before we got an apartment together (it was just one big room with a shared toilet). You simply couldn't find a nicer guy. He was quiet, real honest, and a good student. He was on the way to his first "real job" interview when the accident took place. I'll miss him forever."

Ralph O'Reilly

Annual Family Summary

This section may be optional—the Director already has lots to do—but it's nonetheless a great idea and may be a perfect family Christmas or holiday gift for every member, in gratitude for their participation during that and the preceding years.

An "Annual Family Summary" is just that, a wrap-up in summary form of what occurred during the year of _____. It may be a page or two long (at least in the beginning), probably divided into topics (births, baptisms, graduations, Honor Rolls, marriages, deanships, corporate presidencies, books published, and, alas, deaths—everything but birthdays). It may include prose glad, happy, or sad. The content and design are yours.

It may also be an opportunity for another family member to participate since it's really a one-product process of cutting and pasting the events of that year, reassembling them in some (probably chronological) order by category, and posting the final rendition on a page called "___ SMILES ANNUAL FAMILY SUMMARY." Whether an additional "thank you" copy is then sent by email or snail mail to the family members is, again, a family decision.

Why does this extra page have special historical value? Because it is so much easier to see the family happenings for a year gathered in one place in one consistent, logical form. If that is so, think of how much easier it will be at that time 200 years hence to look back through the family summaries year by year!

Another thing that is very important. It should list in large letters the names (perhaps with photos) of all those directly involved that year in the production and maintenance of the Smiles living family tree, plus a running list, present to past, of the Directors in charge of preserving the heritage. That alone may be reason enough to mail this summary to every family (or member) currently on the living tree.

Sample Annual Family Summary

Annual Smiles Family Summary

2007

This was a fairly quiet year in the Smiles family, except, of course, for Ed Jr. and Ann who gave birth to Edna Louise (Ballou) on February 6, a suppertime baby (6:27 p.m.) weighing 6 pounds and six ounces. Edna is anything but quiet!

Rosa received her A.A. as a med tech this June, which is a great relief to the rest of us in the family who had taken turns being her human pincushions while she dug for veins! She began working part-time with Dr. Al Torres in July.

We had a junior high school graduation in June: Paul was finally released from Jefferson Junior High, and started Park Plaines High in September. Not too many years from now Paul's sisters Belinda and Rita will get their Jefferson release papers too.

The 2007 Smiles Family Honor Roll listed four geniuses bearing our genes: Rita Smiles twice, Tom Ballou (for the 14th time), and Rosa Smiles. (You suppose her kids were doing Rosa's homework?)

Bill got his second hole-in-one, June 13 on the 138-yard sixth hole at Ravenswood Golf Course. His three regular golfing cronies (Lu, Larry, and Ralph) witnessed the miracle. They made him buy lunch and so much beer that Lora had to go drive the four of them home. At 78, he is the second oldest active golfer at the club to score an ace. Bill and Wanda also celebrated their 53rd anniversary—to each other.

Ed and Lora (Ballou) reached their 30th anniversary of wedded bliss, or that's what they're telling the rest of us.

Reginald and Rosa bowled on the championship team in the adult league this fall, and Reggie had his team's highest single game, a 283.

Barry and Dolores vacationed in Costa Rica in April; Lorita is starting her second year in the Peace Corps in Cartagena, Colombia, and Tom cycled 280 miles with three fraternity brothers in Tennessee in August. He ran the 50 and 100 in the spring at Northern Illinois University (ending his eligibility) and won six races, was fourth in the conference final (in 100 meters), and lettered for his second time.

The Smiles Family Reunion was a grand two-day affair in mid-June at the Lions Park Campground and Conference Room in Park Plaines, Illinois. Everybody but Ed Ballou was there (he was speaking at a business conference in New York), and it was a great chance to meet six members of Dolores's family, including Ann Ballou's mother. We laid out the contents of the Family Treasure Box, shot a family video (now available both at the website and as a lender), took turns creating audio CDs (also available at the respective Personal Information Pages), and had a dozen full-family photos taken with

Bill and Wanda. We also put on at least ten pounds since the cooking was catered by Rosa's 100 cousins and uncles, who also provided mariachi and dance music.

Aunt Lydia survived both food poisoning and the shingles during the fall, but managed not to contaminate the rest of us. Otherwise, 2007 was a very healthy year for the Smiles.

Thanks go to those who directed and ran the Smiles Living Family Tree in 2007:

Director: Lora (Smiles) Ballou
Treasurer: Barry Smiles
Board Members: Bill Smiles, Lydia Smiles, Ed Ballou

Family Treasures in Print

Perhaps the easiest things to share with present and future family members are items in print. Most are already halfway to the preservation home if they are in copiable digital format!

What could either be saved in immediately readable and usable Word format or scanned and saved as they ultimately appear in some printed or published form?

- articles
- books
- booklets
- text-based manuscripts
- items about family members
- musical scores or printed artwork by the members
- even diplomas or texts of any kind upon which the family name is proudly placed

Articles and books, or similar published items by the family members, can be saved and shared many ways.

For articles or short works, if you just want the content saved and will accept without seeing a scanned facsimile that the words were indeed printed and made public when the person claims, then a Word file can be the most easily readable stored format, either kept as a linkable download (perhaps with a several-sentence summary, including the publication date, page number[s], and other specifics noted) or converted into Web (.html) text and stored in immediately readable form.

Longer works, like books, are often commercially issued simultaneously in ink-on-paper and digital formats, so in the latter case, the evidence, if you will, is simply sent to the Director in the same digital form, if it is in an easily reachable reading format like Adobe .pdf. In this way a book is kept as a text download, accessible as a link, then reproduced on the reader's computer. If the Director wants the book download-able directly from the website, then it must be converted to Web text. The actual ink-on-print book can be scanned at 300 dpi in TIFF files and stored that way.

However the longer items are replicated, if they have front and back covers, those too can either be reproduced in Adobe .pdf format and stored for easy access or scanned and viewed as TIFF files.

Newspaper clippings by or about family members can be best preserved by scanning. Since newspaper deteriorates and becomes unsalvageable quickly, it is among the first items that should be preserved. (Sometimes, of course, the source itself like a newspaper or magazine is also saved in digital format and accessible in the library. But that's not too handy even if it survives several centuries hence.)

Musical scores and artwork that are flat and undamaged by a flat-bed scanner can also be scanned.

Alas, there is nothing as exciting as holding the actual pro-duction in one's hand, so all of the above means can be done to guarantee that the content will be readable and admired 500 years hence while an actual copy or copies can also be stored in the Family Treasure Box, as explained in the next chapter.

Family Treasure Box

The term "Family Treasure Box" says it all, except that (1) the term "treasure" may have to be further defined and (2) at some point the treasures won't fit into one box.

Details aside, this is where actual, physical things important to the family are kept, with a "contents" page maintained that lists each item in the collection available at all times at the living family tree website.

What kind of physical things? Quilts, artwork, inventions, carvings, actual published books or CDs, ticket stubs to the 1993 Super Bowl in which son Edgar played, grandpa's last pair of glasses, small wooden carvings of Aunt Lucy's hunting dogs, Bob's letter of admission to West Point, a box of coins personally collected by Lynn from every country in South America, a poster and program of Mary appearing in "King Lear," Uncle Ted's Barbershop cummerbund, Alex's Fife and Drum cap, Bev's Salvation Army harmonica…

Note that there may be some overlap with the Family Treasures in Print, like books, the West Point letter, and the poetry program script as well as things like court documents, land patents, old deeds and letters, or naturalization papers. The actual items would be kept in the Family Treasure Box with the printed contents scanned (at 300-600 dpi) and saved elsewhere (so they can be read forever). The physical CDs might likewise be kept here but the contents might be saved and kept in the audio components of your living family tree.

When is a treasure a treasure?

Even more, when does it become a larger Smiles family treasure rather than a personal memento or items kept by the

Immediate family? The latter is simple: when the immediate family donates it to the Family Treasure Box.

Can the box get too full, in the sense that some things are kept and some aren't accepted?

If Buddy, seven, makes 36 twig baskets at Scout camp and sends the entire batch to be kept eternally in the Family Treasure Box, what do you do? Is there a minimum age? A maximum quantity? A limit per person? A guide list of what the box will hold (or what the family will accept)? An arbiter? Who has the final say?

In truth, while one can foresee irreconcilable family feuds and blood vendettas eroding the love lines, these can almost always be calmly resolved and are hardly a reason for not even creating such a potential treasure trove. That's where a Family Board makes so much sense, with the ability to resolve the rare question regarding an item's propriety or acceptability.

What do you do when the "box" won't fit in a box?

That is, of course, a bigger issue. Where will the family valuables be stored?

If the Smiles have an ancestral plantation passed down from father to child and it has a large empty room somewhere near the turret or gable, the problem is solved: a Smiles Family Museum, with the holdings regularly updated on the family website!

Alas, most families are more likely to have a corner in which an actual big box can be stored, dusted off, and brought to the bi-annual family reunion, to be unpacked, its contents displayed and handled, then repacked and returned. So the size of the items accepted may indeed be more important than the number or kind.

Don't some items need special storage?

If we're talking the long haul, some items will require special attention. For example, long-term storage of textiles and paper products and medium-term care of newspapers require an acid-free environment. (See our website for more details and resources about this topic.)

Textiles should be wrapped in acid-free tissue paper and in an acid-free box and stored in a humidity-free environment in a dark place with a fairly even, constant temperature in the 70s.

Paper products should be treated with an acid neutralizing spray and stored flat in an acid-free box. Otherwise, storage for paper is the same as for textiles. Never store anything of value in plastic bags or wraps.

One trick to see if a closet in an unused bedroom will be usable is to place a couple of Graham crackers in the untended storage space for a week. If they are still mostly crisp, the humidity is acceptable. But storage sheds, garages, attics, or basements are never good choices.

Maybe 12 Family Treasure Boxes?

One thought might be that each of the branches would be in charge of creating, maintaining, storing, and updating the listed holdings of its own immediate family riches rather than centrally storing the goods. It would indeed be a Smiles Treasure Box but if there are three or 12 branches, one person in each branch (maybe the Family Board member of that branch) could be in charge of that group's treasure chest. Then all they would do is contact the Director to update the website listing each time a new gem is added. A wee peek at the central website listing might look like this:

SMILES FAMILY TREASURE BOX

Item	Description	Contact Person	Date added	Branch	See
Military bugle	Used in Iraq war by Ed Jr.	Ann Ballou	9/7/05	Ed Ballou Jr.	<u>X</u>
<u>Carved penguin</u>	Cherry, #2 in Kern County Fair 2005, by Candi	Agnes Ballou	3/3/06	Reginald Smiles	

If the family wants to have a digital photo of some (or all) of the Treasure Box items viewable, it might add the "See" box with a link (<u>X</u>) that will lead to a .jpg photo, in this case, of Sgt. Ed Ballou Jr.'s military bugle. (That photo would be provided the same way other photos are sent to the Director.)

It might also be the best way to store and share a short description of each item. Since the photo would be submitted as an attachment to an email, this description or caption plus the box information could be the body of that email.

Or maybe some mixing and matching?

The same idea but some specialization added. Some of the valuable cache will likely be clothing, like uniforms, wedding dresses, or baptism apparel. Perhaps one member of the family is more comfortable or better at keeping textiles cleaned, treated, and properly stored in a large closet, and they would volunteer for that part of the family box. So all clothing items would be sent to them.

And another already has a moisture-free, cool room for another collection and would gladly save part of the room for valuables that must be maintained in just such an environment, rather than in Uncle Elmo's tanning shed.

While the paperwork, like updating the website of new additions and adding a .jpg photo and caption might be maintained by the Director, special items would be kept where they would get the best long-range care. Again, a Family Board would be an asset in this kind of arrangement.

A chance for many more to participate

By decentralizing the Family Treasure Box it gives many more family members an opportunity to directly participate in your living family tree. Better yet, it's far short of heavy lifting or dawn-to-dusk sweat. An occasional item will be added to the collection; a description, caption, and photo must be prepared and submitted, and the item must be added to the storehouse. Every now and then some, or the newest, of the items must be carefully packed, brought, and displayed at the family gathering. And the participant must maintain a modicum of vigil so the kids or babysitter don't "use" or sell the family riches! That's it. An honorable but hardly exhausting personal responsibility that can lead to a truly valuable one-item-at-a-time 1000-year collection.

A parting thought, wherever the valuables are stored: they are to be faithfully returned to the box every time they are removed, to display, share, clean, or use in any way. History and preservation are the operative words!

Family Flashes

Sometimes the family news is so exciting or sad or alarming (like when klutzy cousin Calvin got signed to play pro basketball) that you want to instantly share it with all your kin.

But some of the family members simply don't want to know, even if Chicken Little is 100% right and they are ignorant at their own peril!

Thus "Family Flashes" are for those who care.

They are nothing more than quick memos to a select list of addressees in the Director's email program of family folks who want to know important family news **immediately**, in part because they are curious (a meaner person might say nosy) and in part because it saves them from having to regularly check the living family tree on their computer.

A five-step decision looms:

1. Decide if you want to offer this extra feature at all.
2. If so, choose whether the Director will do it or whether he/she will email the news to another member who will do the mechanical posting and sending.
3. Determine what kind of news gets the instant treatment. For example, births and deaths are top candidates for quick sharing but promotion from deputy assistant floor manager to assistant floor manager, if included in your living family tree at all, can probably wait. So if you want to offer this feature, it's best at the outset to select the topics it will usually cover. (Also allow for a wag window so should something extraordinary occur—like a grandson being chosen to receive a Congressional Medal of Honor—the Director can create an equally extraordinary Family Flash.)

4. Ask all of the family members on the tree if they want to be included in the irregular Family Flashes, explaining why the feature exists, what it looks like, and on what kinds of occasions it will usually be sent, with the assurance that they can always change their mind about being an email recipient.

5. To the Director: create the "send to" list and the simplest of templates so all that you must do is type or cut/paste in the news and load it into another email, then send it. Bingo.

Family Flash information also appears in other ways on the website, though with less urgency. A death will lead to an "In Memoriam" page, a birth will also appear in the "Tip of the Hat" area and the Key Date List, and all of it will eventually wend its way back to and affect the Personal Information Registry.

The Message Sent in a Family Flash

What are you going to send those special souls in the "Smiles Family Flashes" folder?

Let's say that Ann Smiles has just had a baby. The smiling Papa sends you an email giving you the wailing details. You go to a half-blank file in your computer called "Family Flashes template" (we'll see a model in a moment) and you type or cut/paste the facts that Papa sent you into that template and send it to the software provider.

What specific information should a family member submit for a Family Flash?

Often a Family Flash moment is one of great joy or sorrow so it's best just to keep the information to the basics, then if something is missing the Director can ask for more specifics. The shorter it is, the more likely it will be read.

The best guideline: what would *you* like to know about a birth or death or major event? Like, specifically what happened? Answer in your message the six guide words that journalists use: who, what, why, where, when, and how. Include the name (and phone number or email address) of the family member whom others might contact for more details.

This can be sent by email or phoned to the Director. Don't dawdle but do make certain that the facts are correct. (My oldest daughter was born in Ecuador, and when I went to the Embassy the next day to inform them so she would be registered as an American citizen, they asked me how tall she was. Weight I knew, but height, no idea at all. She couldn't even stand. She seemed very little so I said 12", suspecting it was more like 8". The clerk gave me an odd glance but to this day she is officially 12" tall at birth! If you get it wrong with your family, you are in for a life of comedic suffering.)

What do you put on the template?

Not much. It's just a wee file, the shell of permanent information into which the new flash facts are inserted, like this:

SMILES FAMILY FLASH!

(insert the facts here…)

This information was provided by _____. More details will appear soon at the website at the "Tip of the Hat!"

Let's see what the Family Flash announcing Ann and Ed Jr.'s new baby looked like:

SMILES FAMILY FLASH!

Edna Louise Smiles was born at the Roselee Hospital in Lincoln, Wisconsin, last night (2/6/06) at 6:27 p.m., healthy, noisy, and with a wisp of brown hair but no teeth. She weighed 6 lbs. 6 ounces, was 20" long, and said to say hello to the entire family! Parents? Ann and Ed Ballou Jr. For more information, call Grandma Lora at (267) 323-4567.

This information was provided by Lora Smiles. More details will appear soon at the website at the "Tip of the Hat."

All that had to be sent to the Director was the center section, so that was all that the Director had to post, plus the name of who provided the information.

Ancestral
Family Tree

That "old-fashioned family tree" that I mentioned and lauded earlier? This is it, retitled to Ancestral Family Tree, in a fuller-bodied form. (If your "family tree" is in the form of a fan, what follows also applies.)

There are millions of people involved in some aspect of genealogy in the United States alone so there is no reason for me to describe it further on these pages, which are in fact dedicated to a process that, in a way, picks up where traditional family trees leave off.

But a very strong argument can be made that its genealogical findings and methods could lead to an intriguing and valuable component of a future-looking "living family tree."

The core couple of our LFT example is Bill and Wanda Smiles, born respectively in 1928 and 1934. Our project is to build a living memory bank from them and their offspring in which they and each of their progeny can personally record their own written words, voice, photographic image, and video presence.

But what about Bill and Wanda's parents, and their parents, going backward, plus their sisters and brothers, great uncles and aunts, and so on until the roots disappear? That's flat-out family tree digging, except that here we are starting with the end products, Bill Smiles and the former Wanda Lynch, and limiting our dig to their direct descendants.

In a rather simplistic way, the two family trees—the conventional one and our living family tree—would unite and branch forward and backward from Bill and Wanda, like this:

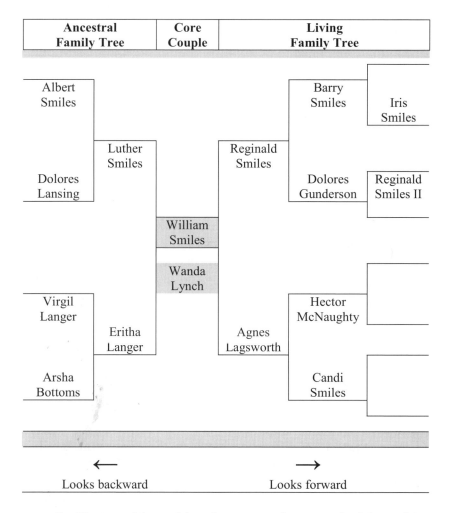

Ancestral Family Tree	Core Couple	Living Family Tree	
			Iris Smiles
Albert Smiles		Barry Smiles	
Luther Smiles		Reginald Smiles	
Dolores Lansing		Dolores Gunderson	Reginald Smiles II
	William Smiles		
	Wanda Lynch		
Virgil Langer		Hector McNaughty	
Eritha Langer		Agnes Lagsworth	
Arsha Bottoms		Candi Smiles	

← Looks backward   → Looks forward

So if we could combine those trees, how much richer a historical heritage would that be for Bill Smiles IV in 2096!

If the traditional family tree (the Ancestral Family Tree in our new context) limited itself just to the usual items—when and where the person in question was born, the children they had (with the names, birth dates, and birth locations of each), and the date of and age at the person's death,—think of how instructive that would be if it extended backward many generations, and what a sense of genetic belonging and solidity that would bring..

But why would we limit ourselves so one-dimensionally? Why not use as many of the "ways" as we can now use for current family contributions?

For example, it's conceivable that one or several of Bill and Wanda's parents are still living, and far more likely that their siblings are pinkly extant. If so, why aren't three-dimensional files being created at the website so our living family tree users a century hence can also see their photos, hear them being interviewed, and see them working in their garden?

Even among the descendants that have passed, photographs (or even paintings) surely are available to be scanned and added to the biographical sketch. And a few might have left audio cassettes or even earlier 78s to add oral history to the recorded facts.

Then there's the half box of historical artefacts that keep being passed down, plus great-uncle Henry's railroad watch. What grand additions to the Family Treasure Box, though each must be clearly labelled and dated before the facts are lost.

Two more thoughts.

One, there is a difference between the "ancestral family tree" and the "living family tree," so attention should be paid to that distinction. The former is an attempt, almost entirely after-the-fact, to create a clear lineage up to the core couple, then to fill in those earlier lines with as much fact and living flesh (through voice and vision) as possible.

The living family tree is an attempt to build a historical presence at varying stages of the family members' lives, and to create some communal presence through things like videos at the reunions. That is an ongoing action, a never-ending play with new characters each living their own plot and sharing slices of it with others living and yet to come.

Two, this component more than any other may require its own leader and champion, if for no other reason than that the Director of the larger project already has a good-sized plate and it's almost full. Better to have a friend in the family do the looking backward, to keep it accurate and report it consistently. That way if either this leader or the LFT Director contacts a family member about some specific action, it will be clear what project they represent and where the results of that request will appear in the larger family historical collective.

That, in turn, will require both of these leaders to work together to design a consistent family website in which all of the components are in harmony in purpose and format.

It would make sense that the "ancestral family tree" leader also prepares a similar submission guide for the items he or she wants sent in, and that that information be included in the regular Family Submission Guide.

Journals, Diaries, and Memoirs

At last, a reason to write journals, diaries, or memoirs, plus a treasured way to keep them visible and appreciated long after you have passed!

Journals and diaries are for immediate use, to preserve thought and observation and give order to one's intimate world. They also provide valuable glimpses into your everyday life that is impossible to get any other way.

Memoirs usually have a grander purpose and scale, a more public hope that others will want to know your story, and even pay big bucks to share it in a best-selling book, then a movie or on TV.

Wouldn't it be great if that memoir dream came true? For most folks, alas, unless they are a celebrity, their writing and insights are extraordinary, and other readers (and a miraculously handy publisher) can't help themselves, memoirs remain that dream.

But not in our scenario. Whichever of the formats you pursue, or some combination or permutation of the three, the results are an historical boon for your grandchildren's grandchildren's grandchildren. Fortunately, your own kids and cousins will read and enjoy them too.

So this chapter will not talk about royalties, call-in talk shows, or agents, rather about you zeroing in on the things, people, and events that will show what a guy or gal living at the opening to the 21st century experienced, saw, felt, and wanted; about hopes, fears, accomplishments, choices, and near misses; about things used, eaten, made, and maybe even invented.

Another important point: while this chapter has spoken of words to be stored digitally, any of the three formats can also be recorded, saved, and enjoyed almost forever orally. That would, at the time of this writing, begin as an audio CD, edited and probably saved in .mp3. But in whatever form, the content is the same. By both means, and others, what is submitted for family sharing should be the very best you can do. That means, for a memoir, a rough draft, some proofing, and a final draft. For a journal or diary, at least attentive editing. Why? So what others read (or hear) is precisely what you want to say both now and after you have joined the family eternal.

"Edit your diary or journal?" you ask. Don't rewrite either, just make them understandable for the ages. Add surnames (and first names) to nicknames, explain or write out abbreviations or "in" jokes or phrases, perhaps tie in an occasional historical reference if something important happened on earth that day…

Right now is a golden time to be a writer, with computers making the recording of your thoughts (particularly the editing) so much easier and faster. It's no surprise that when people reach their late 50s, 60s, and even 70s (or more) the first thing they put on paper is the story of their life.

I've been a publisher and editor for 30+ years so I've literally read hundreds of others' memoirs that they wanted to put in print.

I asked writers what they wanted to have happen with this writing. In other words, less politely, why were they doing it? (That was before memoirs became fully understandable in a living family tree sense.)

In my experience (though I never made a serious tally), maybe a third had sincere expectations of receiving a healthy return from the sale of their manuscript. (None, to my knowledge, ever did.) Perhaps a third more wanted to produce and leave their history to their children—and their children. And the rest had no idea at all but they nonetheless were compelled to get something about themselves on paper to keep a mortal foot on earth before (and after) they took leave.

Memoirs from the last third were usually quite awful. They were rambling, whatever-came-to-mind strings that were vaguely chronological, usually without roots (dates, places, names, historical tie-ins), and shockingly devoid of emotional caring or depth. Kin reading those last manuscripts 100 or 200 years from now would surely have been saddened by and disappointed in their blood-linked elders, and scarcely any wiser about the intricate, exciting challenges the writer had faced in the earliest days of the 2000s.

I suspect, however, that most of the rest who seriously intended to inform family members (or other readers) who followed would have left absorbing insights and exciting accounts, however unpolished their prose might have been. Theirs would have been among the most colorful and entertaining fruit on your living family tree.

How the living family tree solves the problem

A "family living tree" firmly planted provides a framework and rationale, plus the storage, accessibility, and long-term sharing vehicle, that will keep your words and effort vital and easy readable for decades or centuries.

It provides a permanent, specifically designed structure that will integrate your life into your relatives' lives now and into the near and far future. The people in your family are the only reasons for the tree's existence. Their lives, shared, and their stories in their own words are the heart of that tree's trunk. All contain life's lessons told by the members while they are still living. You and they are the true embodiment of hope, success, heartbreak, courage, everyday frailty and weakness, tenacity, love, and laughter.

Earlier, for me, the saddest part of reading personal family histories was the almost certainty that, if the venture was followed to its conclusion (most never went beyond a short chapter), the words would have had a life use of one or two generations, until they were inadvertently (or intentionally) thrown out.

There was no place to store them. No reason to keep them. No tradition of reading them to learn about life, oneself, or one's roots.

Now, with your living family tree that openly invites and encourages diaries, journals, and memoirs, their long digital future is less a concern than the quality of the writing they contain. The hope is that the words and the life behind them convey the full joy, spirit, and being of the person creating them, and that it is evident to every reader and family member.

Some thoughts and guidelines about memoirs

Memoirs are not novels, short stories, or even how-to nonfiction. Life has a predictable plot and we all know how the story inevitably ends. Thus two things are critical here: is what is said true and how well is the story told.

Story? You bet. The most important story a person can share. Yet it needn't be embellished or hyped or reconfigured to alter its own innate excitement and uniqueness. It mostly needs clarity, order, and enough action verbs and picture words to carry us back to the times and events shared.

So, some guidelines (with biases) to make this life sharing a fun, fast, and enriching adventure:

1. Just do it. Tell the world what your life has been like. It's important for your children (and spouse) to know, but progressively more important for future generations. It's also good for you.

2. Do it like a professional writer while you grow into the cloak. Create a sensible outline and attack it one chapter at a time. When you write each chapter, do enough research first to get going. Then write. Forget spelling, syntax, commas. Just get the words down. Go back, add to and double-check the facts, and fill in what you left blank. Finally, edit and edit and edit that chapter until a rock becomes a gem.

3. After all of the chapters are completed, do another edit of the whole thing.

4. Find an objective editor who will mark the errors and slow prose, and who will suggest ways to avoid redundancies and improve the overall structure. Then prepare the final, edited, corrected draft. (Amateurs stop after one inspired draft; professionals put the work through several drafts.)

5. Unless your life was one of non-stop highlights that simply must be retold, zero in on five or eight or ten of the most important activities or elements in your life—you define "important."

6. Names, dates, and places are important—it's not a novel, and accuracy counts—but also remember to inject the sense of action, the spirit, and the visual details. Only you know what happened. You must bring it alive. You must help us see with your eyes, to feel and touch and hear.

7. Share history. What was commonplace when you were young will be almost unimaginable read 100 years hence. I remember sneaking into the milkman's delivery truck to steal pieces of ice to suck. Makes perfect sense to me even now (though I'm not quite sure why I wanted to do it) but almost no sense to my grandchildren who will wonder what the ice was for. And have no idea that the milk came in glass bottles, and the milkman left as much milk as empty bottles indicated.

Will they know that the cream at the top of the milk had to be separated? That milkmen were never women? And that the ice was anything but clean...

8. Don't preach. Who wants to read it? If there is a point or moral to your life, or sections of it, simply tell the story and the message will be obvious.

9. Veracity will always be questioned however honorable you are, so if you claim to have won a gold medal in the Olympics, provide a citation in print where that is confirmed. Or if three of you scaled Mount Peak, who were the other two? Give confirming details where it is important.

10. Remember that in your living family tree you can inject other support items as needed: photos of events or people mentioned, a video short, audio comments from others involved (or yourself), and examples of items mentioned in the Family Treasure Box or scanned directly into the memoir. The goal is a master manuscript that can be downloaded by any family member (or other person) eager to read your words at any time, as is or with illuminating attachments.

You can write a memoir in any order. You can focus on baiting shrimp traps almost forever. You can tell us what you did or didn't do, how you first met your wife (or met your first wife), where you were when President Kennedy or Dr. Martin Luther King were assassinated or when 9/11 took place (and how those with you reacted), the scariest thing you ever did, why you picked your most enjoyable job, what it felt like when your kids were born, all of the autos or horses or houses you have owned (and the fate of each), what was third grade in 1944 like, the best teacher or preacher or coach you ever had (and why). It's your life. Help us relive those days again...

Take a quick look at the next idea (Unforgettable Recollections). It might help you focus on particular key events.

Unforgettable Recollections

A close friend and scrapbook expert, Tamara Lipori, made a great suggestion while reviewing the **Diaries**, **Journals**, and **Memoirs** section. In fact, it's so good it deserves its own chapter.

Tamara pointed to those rare, unforgettable, "where-were-you-when" events (like 9/11) and asked "Why not let family members share their recollection of how it affected them through a short excerpt that would be posted on their living family tree?

How would this most likely happen?

First, something extraordinary would occur. (Fortunately, these are rare since they usually involve assassination, war, or catastrophe.)

Then the Director, probably days later, would ask the family members to share their reaction to the happening with the rest of the family. The Director might ask where the family member was when it happened, how he found out about it, how it immediately affected her, and perhaps what impact it is having (or had if it occurred farther in the past).

The members who wish to would then prepare and send their response. If sent in writing, it might be from a paragraph to several pages long. It might also be a short audio CD or a video or DVD clip. All of the submissions would be posted on the living family tree for the rest of the family to share.

Think of how interesting that would be over time. If our living family tree had begun in the 1860s, for example, we could read our kins' reactions to the just-happened death of President Lincoln, or to the outbreak of World War I, or where they were when Pearl Harbor was attacked. If the living family tree continues into the future for 500 or 1,000 years, wow!

Soon we will read an example of short response.

But why couldn't this be jump started historically? Why wait for a future tragedy?

Surely some family members still have a clear recollection of the December 6 bombing of Pearl Harbor in 1941. That might be a starter. Others will unforgettably recall the end of World War II, the death of President Franklin Delano Roosevelt, and the assassinations of President John Kennedy and Dr. Martin Luther King.

Today would be the day to get those recollections on the site in print, audibly, or visually, both to share with the current family and to get them recorded live to share with the great-great grandkids to come.

An unforgettable recollection

If the Director asked the above questions about President Kennedy, for example, my response would be:

I was the CARE Director on the Colombian coast (Cartagena, Barranquilla, Santa Marta, and San Andrés/Providencia) and happened to be in Bogotá for a conference. Three or four of us were walking to a downtown eatery for lunch when a man came up to us, put out his hand, and said how sorry he was about our President. We were a bit dumbfounded but figured that something was up, and since TV was still fairly new there we diverted to a bar/restaurant; they'd have a set.

Sure enough, when we entered the whole place was silent, glued to the announcements. (President Kennedy had just been declared dead at that point.) We must have looked gringo because almost to a person the customers and waiters (all men) came up and solemnly offered condolences and shook our hands. Many were in tears, and I never felt such sincerity as I did at that moment. We were still unclear about the details so they quickly filled us in, then all were quiet again to watch the set. When we finished eating, they absolutely refused to let us pay for lunch!

We spent that afternoon at the CARE office watching a TV that I heard the night watchman had brought up and installed. For the next two days, before we returned to our respective offices, it was difficult to go far in public without a person from all levels of life coming up and offering his or her kindness.

Many mentioned that they were proud we had had a Catholic president, and two or three asked if that's why he was shot. But Colombia had been (and remains today) in a civil war with more casualties than our Civil War of the 1860s so they were no strangers to violence, and they accepted it as another very sad killing. The condolences and handshakes continued, in decreasing frequency of course, for months.

Naturally we were sad about the tragedy, but it seemed much farther away, thus a kind of detachment interceded. It wasn't until I was back home two years later that I realized the profound impact it had made in the U.S.

To the family member's "Unforgettable Recollection" they would simply add their name and the date submitted, since I presume the Director would include a brief description of the facts of each event under its respective title to inform readers decades or centuries later why this happening had been so memorable at that time.

Scrapbooks

Scrapbooking has been around for a long time. Queen Victoria had one and Mark Twain, an avid lifelong "scrapper," patented the first easy-to-use scrapbook.

There has been a strong resurgence in its popularity in the past decade. Most towns have a scrapbooking store, and most of the megabookstores also have a scrapbooking section.

The living family tree as well as the old-fashioned family tree have different purposes, of course, but what this book proposes can be made easier for scrapbooks because of several excellent books that explain how a digital scrapbook can be planned and technically created. (Check our website for a continually updated bibliography). In those books, newcomers to computer graphics and page construction can find useful how-to guides while seeing in print how the results will most likely appear.

The LFT concept is closest to the "heritage" scrapbook when that is prepared in digital form. The general scrapbooking focus is much more on the composition of the book itself, of capturing a time or person in static form, with the many inventive art forms and designs that can be used to do that best.

Can scrapbooks be created from living family trees?

They sure can. For example, a scrapbook could concentrate on one person, an event, a specific family, or particular family treasures just using the data and other elements already on hand.

If it were a paper-and-paste book, one need only mine the website to select the desired components, then design, compose, and create a dandy scrapbook from them. Already available are the facts for the text, photos, and stills from a video. If the scrapbook were digital, that could be expanded with actual sound and video. Best yet, those scrapbooks can be saved on CDs, DVDs, or online.

Why not create a physical scrapbook about the core couple when, for example, they celebrate their 50th wedding anniversary? Or a special scrapbook about the first family reunion (at which your living family tree was discussed and given a green light)?

Are there six distinct families now in your LFT? Each of those families might be grateful candidates for a "slice-of-life" (sometimes called a "caught-in-the-act") freeze, in scrapbook form.

And if the Family Treasure Box has 50 or 100 (or five) truly unique items that family members and others would like to know about, an actual ink-on-paper book could be written and published (with the costs and travail that implies) or a first-rate scrapbook, in print or digital, might do just as well (and be far less expensive reproducing items in full color).

Might there be some symbiosis here?

The living family tree is a unique concept that stands on its own merits. Not only is it usable on a daily basis, it becomes progressively more usable and valuable in an accumulative sense. That is, its historical and applicable value will increase the longer it is maintained and built into the future.

But it shares roots and operative processes in common with genealogy and scrapbooking, as they are practiced today.

With genealogy, it is a kind of reverse image (going forward rather than backward) that requires the same kind of linking and fact-sharing that will make the LFT results centuries hence look like family trees of old(e). And if an Ancestral

Family Tree is added, that is genealogy pure and simple, expanded in a slightly different way to add as much photography and sound as possible.

With scrapbooking, it is an issue of purpose, scope, and continuity. But many of the same digital tools and desire for photographic clarity and even webpage beauty and balance are there. Plus an important element already well formed: scrapbookers have an instructive structure nationwide that could readily learn the living family tree concepts, expand their present scrapbooking limitations, redesign existing website software, and offer classes and tutorials to LFT practitioners, particularly to the new cadre of Directors.

DNA and Health Concerns

A decade or two back and the thought of including a personal DNA record would have brought a huge laugh, if the person even knew what it is.

It was first available just a few years ago for a tidy million dollars. Now it can be bought for about $1,000, and that will drop and drop as the process for creating a personal record becomes customized and competition intrudes.

Why would a person or a family want DNA records in their living family tree?

For one thing, it will tell if you are all from the same tree! And it can be interpreted to trace the origin of your earliest family members. But equally as important, as we see potential cures being matched to genes, the DNA records tell precisely what genes you have in your body. There will be many more reasons in the future, so let's suggest here that a living family tree is a great place to store a DNA record, since it is digitally visible, can be replicated, and will be available and useful forever.

And presumably, since the DNA of Neanderthals can be determined, if there's a need, it's possible that the DNA of your earlier kin might be available too if the necessary remnants or trace material, like hair or blood, is somewhere available. Thus, those now living might at least leave the vital remnants needed to recreate their DNA, if needed or wanted later, until the price gets within reach.

Health concerns are more immediate, though not unrelated.

Since illnesses or health conditions often follow our bloodlines, it's useful to know which of our kin have those conditions. Diabetes, for example, or a score of other conditions that, if later kin know existed, could be dealt with or even possibly prevented.

So it makes huge sense to include a checklist, with comments, by every living relative that tells what illnesses and health circumstances they face(d), with, if useful, their medical records, X-rays, or other documentation that will or could help kin to come.

Why not also create as much of a record as one can for earlier family members, for the same reason? While some of the items checked may be anecdotal or subjective (was Uncle Bernard really insane?), the medical records or first-hand accounts from spouses and parents (or kids) could prove invaluable 100 or 200 years from now.

And where better to keep these visible and usable for all who are directly affected than in a living family tree?

The most pressing question is what if the person doesn't want a certain condition, or any, made public while they live? There could be family understanding that all private files, as determined by the individuals themselves, could be just that, only available to the Director (or even made available only after the person's death, or so many years later). Yet to be useful for later kin, it should be clearly stated at what point and under what life-affecting conditions those files could be opened or at least viewable for a specific purpose. Sounds like another decision for a Family Board.

Other Attachments

It's *your* living family tree. Hang on it any new attachments or sections that you wish. We have suggested more than a dozen rather obvious components in this book section, but your imagination (and needs) may well suggest another dozen, or 65, to join or replace our suggestions. That's great. Your tree won't achieve its fullest growth until it blooms in your family genius.

1. For example (an odd example first), If you are the eggplant emperor of Kentucky (or America), that suggests a unique, extra chapter around **eggplants**. Perhaps a new historical unit, a sort of booklet (with text and photos) about the family's involvement with eggplants proudly made available to every family member now, and later updated by future family eggplant-interested members.

2. Is **sports** your family thing? You may want more emphasis put on sports than what otherwise already appears in the Personal Information Repository or at the "Tip of the Hat!" section on special occasions.

A special sports section might list every sports team (and affiliation, like the Scranton Little League; Happy High School in Bullhead, MS, or the Rock Island Chips of the Chester Mountain League [San Diego Padres Class C minor league]) on which a family member played. It might include the sport, position played, dates of participation on the team, and a maximum 30-word highlight summary.

Another section might list family records by sport, with all the necessary details. Three examples:

- **Golf**, hole-in-one: Bill Smiles, 6/13/2007, 138-yard sixth hole at Ravenswood Golf Course. Bill's second hole-in-one; he is the second oldest active golfer at the club to score an ace.

- **Running** (100-meter dash), Tom Ballou, 10:27.33 on 3/27/2007, for Northern Illinois University against Southern Illinois University, at DeKalb. This was his third of six wins in his senior year for NIU, and Tom's fastest time at that distance in college.
- **Bowling**, 283, 9/26/2007, by Reginald Smiles in Adult Bowling League at Holiday Bowl in Park Plaines, Illinois.

To encourage more family members to challenge the best times and scores, the lists might be further defined by gender and by age (under 12, 12-18, 19-30, 31-40, 41-50, 51-60, 61-70, 71+), and then even further subdivided if necessary.

3. Maybe it's **politics** rather than (or in addition to) sports for your clan. So here you would list every political position (elected or appointed) in which a family member served, with details (and perhaps another 30 or so words of highlights or accomplishments achieved).

Do you list the positions they ran for but were defeated? Two thoughts: a Family Board decision or leave it up to the candidates themselves, with the option of listing them or not.

Another angle, perhaps, rather than politics as the theme, would be **public service**. That would include politicians plus city managers, police or fire, school board, recreation directors, or hundreds of others.

Or would **community service** work? In addition to the above, add in a hundred more, like Scout leaders, outreach counsellors, and Peace Corps volunteers.

What about artists, Barbershoppers, band members, actors, choir singers?

4. Many families particularly encourage **educational achievements**, so those might be given additional prominence by having a section or chapter specifically dedicated to that theme.

There, every academic success would be properly listed by name, degree, institution, and date, starting with high school graduation (or G.E.D.). Later, areas of specialization at post-secondary institutions would be added, and dissertation titles listed. These would also include similar achievements in trade, professional, and specialty institutions.

5. Why not **travel**? Perhaps include a map of the Americas, or the world, and let every family member put electronic dots (a different color per member or numbers leading to a key chart, with the person's name) of places visited.

Or different pages for each continent, where the person lists the country and key cities visited, with the date. Why not let them add a short description or commentary about the key spots? Or even add photos that could be linked to the database of photos at the mother website.

Why? To share the adventuresome spirit with kin, but also to be available to discuss places that others may be considering visiting, for tips or suggestions or even precautions…

You get the idea. What's important to you, your immediate family, and those who will follow? Just create the needed or desired extra attachments to give your tree better balance or more brilliance.

Index